From the Texas Cotton Fields to the United States Tax Court

The Life Journey of Juan F. Vasquez

By Mary Theresa Vasquez and Anthony Head

AMERICAN BAR ASSOCIATION
Tax Section

Cover image: From *Los Piscadores,* by Jesse Treviño. Used by permission.

Printed in the United States of America.

Published by the American Bar Association Section of Taxation, 1050 Connecticut Ave. NW, Suite 400, Washington, DC 20036.

Soft Cover 13-Digit ISBN: 978-1-64105-821-6
Hard Cover 13-Digit ISBN: 978-1-64105-820-9
E-Book 13-Digit ISBN: 978-1-64105-822-3

For more information, contact the ABA Service Center at (800) 285-2221 and request product code 5470832 or visit www.ShopABA.org.

This book is dedicated to my grandchildren, Claire Amelia, Maryn Graciela, Juan Flores Vasquez III (Juan Tres), Lauren Olivia, Daniella Vasquez, and Viviana Vasquez (due November 2020).

This book is also dedicated to the children of the world. Remember, to succeed you must "*Sume la bota.*"

—Mary Theresa Vasquez

Working on Juan's story has stirred my mind with many wonderful remembrances of my grandfathers, Marvin Head and Joe Mattingly, who were known to pass along a little of their own wisdom from time to time. To their memory I dedicate this book.

—Anthony Head

Table of Contents

FOREWORD

Connecting the Stories

Connection. That is a principal theme that comes to mind when I contemplate the remarkable life of Judge Juan F. Vasquez. Connection to his upbringing in South Texas, where he labored alongside his grandfather in the cotton fields. Connection to the Mexican American community that makes that region so vibrant. Connection to his family and to his wife, Terry, in particular. (Indeed, it is difficult to contemplate Judge Vasquez's journey through life in the absence of his co-venturer and chief advocate.) Connection to the individuals who believed in him and the schools that helped him realize his full promise. Connection to his present and former law clerks (of which I am one), whom he treats as members of his extended family.

And his connection to members of the federal tax bar, including government attorneys and counsel for taxpayers. As he has walked in both sets of shoes, he genuinely respects the contributions of both to our judicial system. That appreciation is why, at any given tax conference, you are virtually certain to find him in conversation in the hallways rather than in any particular session.

Judge Vasquez's level of connection to the communities and cultures that have shaped his life is not one of obligation. Rather, it is one of pride. His journey from toiling as a young boy migrant worker under the blistering South Texas sun to being sworn in as a Judge of the United States Tax Court would be difficult to believe had it not actually happened. As beautifully chronicled in this text, that journey is marked by optimism, determination, fortitude, and, as with any success story of this caliber, good fortune.

Importantly, I cannot imagine that Judge Vasquez views his past as something he has *overcome* to be where he is today. Rather, he embodies that past, and he celebrates it—joyously. It is one of the reasons the Jesse Treviño portrait of him alongside his grandfather in the fields (*Los Piscadores*) hangs so prominently in his chambers.

I came to know Judge Vasquez well into his lifetime journey, several years after he became the first judge of Hispanic descent to serve on the United States Tax Court. But the unique perspective he brought to the bench is by no means limited to his ethnicity. Many Tax Court judges come to that position following service on Capitol Hill, either from the Joint Committee on Taxation or one of the House or Senate tax-writing legislative committees, or from service within the Internal Revenue Service or the Treasury Department. While some come from a practice representing individuals or corporations in connection with tax matters, few if any have the experience of serving individual clients as a solo practitioner. Judge Vasquez brought to the bench that perspective, one that has given him considerable empathy not only for the individuals pursuing their cases before him but for their attorneys as well.

From my time in Judge Vasquez's chambers, I believe the aspect of his job that he found most enjoyable was being on the road in a range of cities conducting trial sessions. These sessions allowed him to connect with the public that the Tax Court serves as well as with the tax professionals in that particular community. He was, and remains, a man of the people.

I want to share a few of the many stories from my time serving as Judge Vasquez's law clerk, stories that shed light on his personality and character. Even the tale of my hiring is insightful. Although I believe I possessed a number of qualities that would make me a competitive candidate for the clerkship, I do not believe any of those truly mattered in the interview. Rather, it was the first item I listed as an interest at the bottom of my résumé, Texas barbeque. That item led to a discussion of my high school years, when I had moved to New Braunfels, Texas, with my mother to live with my grandparents. During those summers, I worked at a popular waterpark in the area, one that Judge Vasquez had occasionally visited with his family. That pretty much sealed it. He called early the next morning to make me an offer, and in that manner, my high school summer job ended up landing me one of the most personally and professionally fulfilling positions I have ever held.

During my clerkship, I recall one conversation in particular with Judge Vasquez in his chambers that concerned a wave of states adopting lotteries to finance a range of government expenditures, typically education, to make the prospect of state-run gambling more palatable. I expressed my disdain for the idea, not on moral grounds, but instead on the practical distribution of the burden of raising revenue in this manner. These lotteries resembled regressive taxes, given the socioeconomic status of the participants. In a somewhat callous manner, I described how disappointing it was to see people of limited means "blowing" their money on lottery tickets. Later that day, Judge Vasquez returned to this topic with me. He conveyed that what many of these people were buying with those tickets was hope. Hope that they would be freed from their otherwise intractable financial troubles. The prospect of abundance, even if fleeting, provided a source of joy that otherwise would not exist. That conversation provided an important lesson in being slow to judge the actions of others without considering their situation or perspective. Judge

Vasquez has the perspective, indeed the benefit, of not living a privileged life. Charmed perhaps, but not privileged. The empathy generated by his perspective and background is one of his finest qualities as a judge.

This last story is one that provides me with warmth and support to this day. One of my goals in pursuing my LL.M. degree in taxation at New York University was to pursue a career as a legal academic. Shortly into my clerkship with Judge Vasquez, that opportunity arose. My former NYU professors inquired about my interest in serving as an acting assistant professor in the program, a temporary position that almost certainly would lead to a permanent job in the field. The position was to commence at the conclusion of my first year as a clerk in Judge Vasquez's chambers. Yet, I had committed to serving as his clerk for a two-year term. After having passed on a similar opportunity immediately after graduation, I doubted many more opportunities of this caliber would come along. So, with a high degree of anxiety and borderline nausea, I decided to broach the idea with Judge Vasquez. I arranged for us to grab lunch the next day at Capital Q, a small Texas barbeque joint in the Chinatown neighborhood of Washington, D.C., where I and my fellow clerks at the Tax Court often ate. It was crowded at lunch, and I can remember taking our food to a barstool counter facing the wall adorned with portraits of Texas politicians, with a roll of paper towels (napkin substitute) between us. I can hear his voice now. "So, Brant, what did you want to talk about?"

I shared with him what I had in mind and braced myself for a reaction of disappointment: I received exactly the opposite. Judge Vasquez was ecstatic, viewing this as a wonderful development. He was proud that one of his clerks would be teaching in the NYU program, his alma mater. More broadly, I believe he recognized that teaching was a meaningful goal of mine, one that was by no means easy to achieve. I also believe he appreciated the degree of naïve optimism and ambition I had in pursuing this goal. I came to the conversation anxious, and I left energized and emboldened by his full-throttled support. That conversation captured for me the essence of Judge Vasquez, and I am sure some readers of this book will have their own seemingly regular but poignant experiences with him that capture the pleasure he takes in seeing others succeed. It is a tremendous quality.

This book explores Judge Vasquez's remarkable life. While the juxtaposition of his upbringing and his professional accomplishments is staggering, Juan F. Vasquez–the man, the husband, the father, the friend, the mentor, the judge–cannot be captured by the endpoints of this spectrum alone. Rather, the optimism, determination, gratitude, decency, and joy for life he displayed along the way are what truly capture his greatness.

—Brant J. Hellwig
Dean of the School of Law
Washington and Lee University

Note on Authorship

Mary Theresa (Terry) Vasquez had been compiling materials and was already writing this biography of her husband, Juan Flores Vasquez, when I met them both in March 2013. I was actually researching a biography of San Antonio artist Jesse Treviño and had driven to Houston to interview Terry and Juan, since they had been close friends with the artist since 1982. As it turned out, we all hit it off pretty well. In addition to providing valuable information for my project, Terry and Juan became enthusiastic supporters of the book, which was published in 2019.

At some point, Terry asked if I would be interested in collaborating on Juan's biography. Having already learned much about Juan's life, I thought it would be a great project. After reading through the research archive and interviewing some of Juan's colleagues, it became readily apparent to me that, in her humility, Terry had mostly neglected to include information on her role in supporting Juan's career. The story would simply be incomplete without readers understanding how Terry and Juan have acted as a team ever since they met in high school, and it is not hyperbole to suggest that Juan's success hinged on Terry being in his life.

To rectify the situation, I handled the editorial sections that included Terry and wrote about her in the same third-person manner as other people cited within these pages. This allows for a richer portrait of Juan's life to be written without changing Terry's role as coauthor of the book.

—Anthony Head

Note on the Manuscript

Although some members of the United States Tax Court have provided spoken, written, or emailed information for inclusion in this biography, the content of the book is solely the responsibility of authors Mary Theresa Vasquez and Anthony Head and must not be taken to reflect the views of the Court, any of its judges, or any of its opinions.

CHAPTER ONE

Early Movements

When the light hit the painted image of Judge Juan F. Vasquez's face, the glow also illuminated a few of the other faces that appeared around him on the wall. Titled *American Dream*, the enormous artwork of which Juan was now a part of spreads across two walls and a bit of the ceiling of Mi Tierra Café y Panadería, one of San Antonio's iconic Tex-Mex restaurants, and it showcases the men and women who fought for equal access to the opportunities that make life better in this country, or who excelled at a particular art or talent, or who supported the Hispanic and Latino communities in some unique way. The mural represents those who distinguished themselves, those who stood out, those who made a difference. Juan was in very good company, and from this day forward, he would look out from this sea of painted faces, each of them happy and determined, confident and grateful, just like his.

This all took place on November 14, 2014, in Mi Tierra's busy back dining room. Owned by the Cortez family since 1941, Mi Tierra has long been an anchor of San Antonio's historic Mercado District, a part of downtown where some of the Mexican American population set up businesses and immigrating families from Mexico spread to neighborhoods in the western part of this beautiful Texas city, creating what was then called the Mexican quarter[1] but today is known as the West Side.

Inside the sizable restaurant, it feels like Christmas every day, with shiny holiday ornamentation hung year-round. There are strolling musicians and colorful *picado* flags flapping overhead. The walls are lined with old photos of San Antonio along with paintings from local artists. The savory aromas from a never-ending parade of platters of cheese enchiladas, sizzling beef fajitas, and baked *cabrito* (young goat, the "Monterrey Special") fill the bustling restaurant.

As the unveiling ceremony commenced, and when Juan's name was announced and his portrait on the wall was lit up by a spotlight, there was an acknowledgment of some of his professional achievements as well as some interesting aspects of his life as a native son of San Antonio. He smiled humbly and then he turned to his wife, Terry, and they both enjoyed a quiet moment—a moment of knowing just how much they had achieved together.

Other thin beams of light shone on different, new faces added to the wall, and there was more applause for the others in the audience who were also being honored that day. A feeling of community pride filled the room as the overhead lights came up, illuminating the rest of the mural, which features dozens of greatly admired people—business leaders, artists, musicians, politicians, veterans—who have left their mark on San Antonio.

Originally the idea of Jorge Cortez, Mi Tierra's co-owner, *American Dream* was begun in 1978 by Mexican artist Jesus Diaz Garza as a tribute to the restaurant's founders and Jorge Cortez's parents, Pedro and Cruz Cortez, as well as field laborers and farmers who sold their produce at the nearby farmers' market.[2] After Garza's death, San Antonio artist Robert Ytuarte assumed responsibility for the mural's upkeep in 2000. More than 200 people appear in the mural, including Henry B. González, who fought locally and in the U.S. House of Representatives to balance the cultural and governmental systems to include minorities; former mayor of San Antonio and Housing and Urban Development Secretary Henry G. Cisneros; groundbreaking Tex-Mex musician Flaco Jiménez; actor and comedian (and serious art collector) Richard Anthony "Cheech" Marin; and internationally renowned Mexican artists Diego Rivera and Frida Kahlo.

Since the mural was started, it has become a point of pride to be included, which is why Juan Vasquez remarked shortly after his induction ceremony that it was among the highest honors he'd received. "I knew lots of people on the wall," he recalled. "[Advertising executive] Lionel Sosa, [artist and muralist] Jesse Treviño, [actor] James Olmos, [U.S. congressman] Frank Tejeda, and [icon of the Mexican American Civil Rights movement] César Chávez—to see these people on the wall was very inspirational. It's one of the most wonderful honors you can receive, to be honored by your hometown. I've often said, sometimes you have to earn state, regional, and national recognition before your hometown recognizes you. There's nothing wrong with that, but when your hometown honors you, it's special."

Juan had, indeed, already been recognized statewide, regionally, and nationally. He had, in fact, broken new ground by being the first Hispanic member of the United States Tax Court, a highly specialized federal court comprising experts in the field of taxation dedicated to adjudicating disputes that individuals or companies have with the federal government concerning their tax liabilities. But it had been a long road to eventually receiving this singular honor from his hometown, and it was a road marked with a few bumps in it, especially early in Juan's journey.

Shortly after Juan's birth in San Antonio on June 24, 1948, to José Resendez Vasquez and Amelia Flores Vasquez, his mother began coughing up blood. Not long after Juan's mother was admitted to a hospital, José Vasquez decided that he wasn't up to the job of parenting alone. Baby Juan and his three siblings were taken to live with his father's parents.

Then suddenly, Juan's father agreed to allow Juan's two brothers, José Jr. and Raymundo, and their sister, Sylvia, to live across town with Amelia's parents. But Juan was to remain with José's parents, totally separated from his siblings. "I didn't see them again for many years," said Juan. "So I grew up as the baby with my [Vasquez] grandparents in a two-room house on San Antonio's West Side."

Juan's paternal grandmother, Victoria Resendez, was born in Aramberri, Nuevo León, Mexico, on July 28, 1899. She moved to Texas with her family during the Mexican Revolution, which began in 1910. After marrying Juan Reyes Vasquez in 1920, she raised five children, Emma, José, Antonio, Juanita, and Miguél, while also helping raise Juan and two other grandchildren, Tony and Oscar.

"She raised me as one of her very own, and I did not know that I was a grandchild," said Juan. "She was the typical Mexican American woman whose job was to cook and clean, and raise, love, and discipline children, and at the same time be a wife. She never complained about these responsibilities that I know of."

Juan's grandfather, Juan Reyes Vasquez, was born in San Antonio on June 26, 1898. He joined the U.S. Army in July of 1918; was inducted at Camp Travis, now part of Fort Sam Houston; and trained at Camp Sheridan in Montgomery, Alabama. For most of the duration, he served in the 378th Bakery Company of the Quarter Master Corps. Because World War I ended in November of that year, Juan R. Vasquez didn't see any action, nor was he sent overseas. After the army, he went to work at the Bexar County Court House as a part-time deputy constable and also sold life insurance in San Antonio and South Texas.

Located on South Laredo Street, the Vasquez's rental house, had an outhouse in the backyard. The front room of the house was the dirt-floor bedroom, and Juan's grandmother, whom he called "Ama," was constantly sweeping it. The back room was the kitchen with a wooden floor and a wood-burning stove. There was only cold running water; Ama warmed up water on the stove for cooking and bathing. Kerosene lamps were used to light the nights.

Because there was no electricity, the family had an ice-box rather than a refrigerator. In those days the ice-delivery truck was a daily sight in the many West Side neighborhoods. Typically, a young boy on the truck yelled, *"Hielo, hielo, se vende hielo. Quién quiere comprar el hielo?* (Ice, ice, ice for sale. Who wants to buy ice?)" as it drove up and down the streets. Juan's grandparents bought ice every day. With no refrigeration, groceries too were replenished daily. Ama often sent young Juan—"Juanito" to most of his friends and family—across the street to the Don Fermin store to buy groceries *en fiado* (on credit).

The backyard often flooded because it and other low-lying parts of the neighborhood were the regular victims of rising waters of nearby Salado Creek and Elmendorf Creek. The family sometimes retreated to a relative's house nearby to wait out the floods.

Looking back, with the benefit of history to guide him, Juan believed these floods were due to the lack of funding from the city for the poorer sections of town: "In those days, there was no Mexican American representation on the city council because the members were not elected by the districts they lived in, but elected city-wide. As a result, there were no funds voted for flood control in these neighborhoods. We were lucky, but there were a lot of families that lost all or most of their household goods whenever it flooded."

In addition to living near these sometimes dangerous creeks, Juan lived within walking distance of two slaughterhouses and packinghouses (one for pigs, the other for horses). The offensive smells from those operations came to be a normal part of growing up in that neighborhood. More importantly, those meat-processing businesses were a major employer to a lot of people, including some of Juan's family, and they helped keep the neighborhood's financial situation a little more stable.

Juan can also remember that there were many cantinas nearby, which his grandfather, Juan R. Vasquez, "Apa," frequented. As long as Apa was spending time with Juan—no matter the circumstances—Ama wouldn't get upset with her husband; she was always concerned that her husband never neglect his grandson. Apa's favorite bar was Solis, a place with spittoons and a long wooden bar with a railing where men could place their feet as they drank beer and spat tobacco. Throughout his life, Juan could easily recall visiting this particular bar because his grandpa took him there so often.

But they stopped by other neighborhood bars, too, almost nightly. Sometimes Apa told Juan to "stay in the car," which wasn't a fun way to pass the evening. Other times Juan accompanied his grandfather inside, where there were snacks and sodas. In time, Juan discovered that "my grandfather had the habit of drinking and cussing, and I acquired the habit of cussing. At that young age of four or five, I did not know any better. The men at the bars thought it was funny. My grandfather would smile and hug me with approval and say, *'Este es mijo'* (This is my son). I did not know those cuss words were not acceptable language until I moved into my mother's house several years later."

Juan's impression of his grandfather was—in a good sense—that of a man who "hustled" to feed his family. For instance, Juan R. Vasquez also made money by helping out families in the neighborhood who were provided food rations, like cornmeal, powered box milk, and canned ham. Many of the neighbors didn't have transportation to pick up their subsistence; so Juan's grandfather, who had a car, drove them to the city's distribution centers and, in turn, he would be paid (for the gas and his time) with some of their rations. He then sold these products to farmers to feed their pigs. He also repaired watches and sold fresh, local produce from the back of his car. All the while, his very young grandson Juan was noticing that industrious spirit, and learning firsthand how it's just fine to always be trying to improve your situation.

"Apa always provided for his family. I was never hungry," Juan said. "I looked to him as a father, and I enjoyed his love and affection and hugs even if they were at the cantinas."

As for his grandmother, Juan said, "she was truly a mother to me, who loved me and cared for me. My aunt Janie said that my grandmother Vasquez cried a lot after I was removed from her home by my biological mother in 1955. I had lived with my grandparents from the age of six months to seven years old."

CHAPTER TWO

Getting to Know One's Mother

The hospital to which Amelia Flores Vasquez was taken when her youngest son, Juan, was a baby was actually a tuberculosis sanatorium, located in Carlsbad, Texas, near San Angelo, about 450 miles northwest of San Antonio. Although she didn't know it at the time, Amelia would spend the rest of her life battling tuberculosis.

Amelia Flores, born on September 16, 1923, in San Antonio, was the second of Jesus Jimenez Flores and Basilia Hernandez Flores's 14 children. (A 15th died in infancy.) The Flores family moved around South Texas because Jesus and Basilia were migrant workers, picking crops, mostly cotton, to provide for their livelihood. The children, too, were expected to work and Amelia picked cotton until she met José Vasquez in 1941, probably at a dance in San Antonio.

José Resendez Vasquez was born on March 22, 1922, in San Antonio. Not much is known about his early life, but he married Amelia Flores on December 9, 1941, two days after Pearl Harbor was bombed and U.S. participation in World War II began.

"My dad served in the army as a firefighter in the 1949th Engineering Aviation Battalion and was honorably discharged," Juan said of José Vasquez. "I have been told that he was discharged because he had some psychological problems as a result of his position as a firefighter. I now wonder if he had post-traumatic stress syndrome, which was not recognized and, of course, there was no treatment for this condition in those days."

Certainly, that could have been at least part of the reason for José Vasquez taking his kids to his parents' house to live after his wife became ill and was sent to the sanatorium.

"Dear Children," Amelia Vasquez wrote on September 4, 1950. "I your mother 'Amelia' will explain [to] you all that sometime back ago I was declared a sick person of a dreadful sickness, and it meant for me death for sure or go to a Sanitarium to get well. My heart was so broken cause I had to leave you all, but I wanted to get well for you'll, and you'lls future welfare was my only concern, so that's why I left you all, so someday when God from up above claims me, never feel sorrow."[1] The letter was postmarked from Sanatorium, Texas.

According to the *Handbook of Texas*, Amelia's sanatorium was originally called Anti-Tuberculosis Colony No. 1 when it opened in 1912 as the first institution of its kind in the state. The 57-bed facility was renamed State Tuberculosis Sanatorium in 1913 and grew to accommodate the seemingly never-ending numbers of tuberculosis patients in Texas. By the time Amelia arrived on April 4, 1950, there were around 900 beds. The whole facility had grown so large, in fact, that it practically became its own self-sufficient civic entity. In addition to having a post office, there was a school, a hog farm and butcher shop, and a printing press that published the sanatorium's own newspaper, the *Chaser*.

Most patients were expected to stay about six to nine months for treatment. Amelia Vasquez frequently stayed for many months at a time over seven years. (In 1951, the facility was renamed the McKnight State Sanatorium, for a previous superintendent.) Whenever she returned to San Antonio, Amelia lived with her parents and three of her children—only she had to live separately from them, in the back shack of the house.

Tuberculosis, also known as consumption, is contagious. It spreads through the air from person to person, and usually afflicts the lungs. It is marked by a constant cough (including coughing up blood), fever, fatigue, and weight loss. Antibiotics generally make tuberculosis much more curable now, but when Amelia Vasquez suffered from it, its treatment was still early in the antibiotic era. Apparently, she never was cured because during her stays with her parents she couldn't spend time with her youngest son, Juan. Both sets of grandparents were too afraid for the child's health to allow a visit.

In 1955, when Amelia again left the sanatorium and returned to San Antonio, she began to try again to reclaim her life. At some point during the five years that she was back and forth from Carlsbad, she and José Vasquez divorced.

"I learned my mother was forced to divorce my dad so that she could get child support, public welfare, from the city. She filed charges of 'no child support' or 'child desertion' against him, and he was jailed," Juan explained. "The city gave my mother $40 per month as income. I truly, honestly believe that my mother still loved my dad but she had no choice."

The family lived in a small home on Pecos Alley on the West Side. The tiny wooden house had a wood floor. They had a small black-and-white Philco television set, though it was often broken, and there was a radio. "My mother had a crush on Elvis, and she seemed happy each time she heard his music. My mother even went to the neighbors to watch Elvis sing on *The Ed Sullivan Show*, and she was very happy when she came back to the house," said Juan.

"She also loved Humphrey Bogart," said José Vasquez Jr., Juan's oldest brother. "She loved Elvis and a lot of the movie stars of the '50s, but she really loved Humphrey Bogart."

Despite her adoration for Bogey and the King of Rock and Roll, Amelia was a devout Catholic and she took her kids to church every Sunday, sitting right in the front pew of Immaculate Heart of Mary. The lessons from the pulpit didn't always stick with her children, however, especially her youngest son, who often found himself put in the corner or knocked on the head with his mother's knuckles (Juan would remember these light raps on the head as "*cocanotes*") after he talked back or cussed in Spanish, a behavior he'd learned from living with his grandfather Vasquez.

"My mother had a very difficult time with me and was determined to convert me," Juan said. "I guess I was surprised that she scolded me as much as she did because it had been funny whenever I cussed around my grandfather. I did not know her as a real *loving* mom. I do feel that I longed for a real mother—but it was okay because my grandmother Vasquez was a loving mother figure."

José Jr. remembered his kid brother was pretty normal, despite needing a little time to adjust to his new surroundings. "He acted a little spoiled when he first came back from my grandparents," he said. "But he was a good kid. I think I got into a lot more mischief than he did, actually."

It's important to know that Juan, who was about seven years old at the time, had no memories of his mother or siblings before living with them. At first, he couldn't understand why he was suddenly living with this woman and her children; so naturally it would take some time to feel like part of the family. Juan recalled his sister, Sylvia, tried to protect him from his mother's heavy hand of discipline by sometimes speaking up, but, as he remembered, Sylvia often received a lecture to mind her own business.

This is not to suggest that Juan was living a lousy childhood. Although he never had many toys, he often played behind the house, which was surrounded by woods. There were many children to play with in the alley, as well. Juan was a small, scrawny boy, but never felt deterred from doing anything that older, bigger kids did. "I remember having a lot of fun and keeping ourselves entertained. One day, for instance, I was playing outside with the neighborhood children, and we were playing in a mud hole. We made cars out of mud because we had no toys," Juan said.

Things were certainly difficult for Amelia. She was raising four children on her own while holding down two jobs, one as a sales clerk at La Feria, a nearby department store, and the other as a member of the "mama patrol," a crossing guard program for the neighborhood school, Navarro Elementary. José Jr. recalls how his mother tried valiantly for her family but that her efforts worked against her own health concerns. "She was a loving mother, but things were hard. Tuberculosis was hard to cure back then, and she really wasn't supposed to be doing any heavy work," he said.

"She looked really official with the uniform that she wore, and I recall that we were all very proud of her," Juan said. "But I also remember that my mother looked sickly and frail."

Juan had gone from a situation in which he'd always known food was going to be on the table to sometimes being desperate to eat as he grew. Once, he found some peanuts on the floor and hid them in the doghouse—the family had no dog, so it was relatively safe, he thought. But his mother caught him later eating them. She didn't say anything, nor did she take them away, but her tears at the sight confused and saddened him.

For two years, which included moving to another house on New Mexico Alley, Juan learned how to live without what some of the other boys in his neighborhood enjoyed, like new clothes and toys, instead of hand-me-downs, and being able to join the Cub Scouts (Amelia couldn't afford the $1 registration fee). The family struggled, but Juan never realized he was "poor" until he got a little older.

Once, when he was with his friends, Juan stood in front of a movie theater and put out his hand, just like he'd seen other people do. A few pennies made their way to his palm, but somehow word got back to his mother, who was waiting for him when he returned home. He was scolded with a stern verbal warning: "Begging I do not approve of!"

Another time, in a movie theater, Juan was hungry but had no money. "So we looked on the floor and picked up the dropped popcorn and ate it. It was a little smashed but it still tasted like popcorn. I also picked up a hard chocolate candy from the floor and ate it, but then spit it out because it had some hair on it," said Juan.

With her faith and sheer determination, Amelia managed to do her best for her family for the remainder of her life, which was only a couple of years. Juan and his siblings would not have nearly enough time with their mother. By November 1957 she was quite sick again, very weak, and coughing a lot. Trying to be a careful mother, she sterilized all her dishes and everything that she touched. Later that year, when she began spitting and coughing up blood, Sylvia went to the neighbor's house to call her maternal grandparents, who then called for medical help.

"I was told by Sylvia that our mother was picked up by an ambulance, which took her to the hospital. We never saw her again," Juan said.

Amelia Flores Vasquez died on November 10, 1957, at the age of 34. José Jr. was 14 years old, Sylvia was 12, Raymundo was 10, and Juan was 9.

"My mother's death was very confusing to me, and I did not know how to feel," Juan said. "Her siblings, my aunts and uncles, were very sympathetic, and I remember them crying, but I did not understand as I was very young. I only lived with her for two years, and those were very turbulent years."

Although brief with her time, Juan's mother would remain with him in memory all his life. He would sometimes speak of her passing, always with so much sincerity that few seldom forgot about her, and some even could tell her story themselves, like when his future friend and mentor Professor Ira Shepard spoke of Amelia at Juan's federal judicial induction ceremony nearly 40 years after her death.

CHAPTER THREE

The Cotton-Picking Days of Summer

After his mother's death, and with his father essentially out of the picture, Juan was sent with his brothers and sister to live with their mother's parents, Jesus and Basilia Flores.

Jesus Jimenez Flores was born in Sabinas Hidalgo, Nuevo León, Mexico, on July 25, 1895, and came to the United States as a teenager on July 10, 1910, through the border-crossing point at Laredo, Texas. Part of a mass exodus around the Mexican Revolution, he was escaping that country's civil war and looking for a better way of life.

Basilia Hernandez was born in San Marcos, Texas, on June 14, 1904. At the age of 15, she married Jesus Flores, 24, on February 5, 1920, in San Antonio. They had Jesus Jr. in 1921, Amelia in 1923, and Guadalupe in 1925. Shortly afterward, the family migrated to Lubbock because Jesus had heard that the cotton industry there was growing. They stayed about a year and then moved to Branchville and began sharecropping. The family kept growing as well (including children Dolores, Adolfo, Frances, Maria, Pedro, Armando, and Rosa) until a severe drought forced them to leave the area in 1940. The Floreses had another three children (Socorro, José, and Salvador) while living in Pharr, located in the Rio Grande Valley, where the family picked tomatoes, celery, onions, parsley, and lettuce. Sometime in the late 1940s they moved back to San Antonio, where the family bought a house and Basilia gave birth to her final child, Juan.

The two-bedroom house, located on the east side, was about 1,370 square feet, with one bathroom and a small kitchen. When 9-year-old Juan Vasquez arrived with his siblings to live with the Flores family in November 1957, there were already many children living there, as well as kids from other relatives, and even some other grandchildren, including his cousin Loy.

Although José Jr., Sylvia, and Raymundo had previously lived there, the move was another big adjustment for Juan. He'd just been living in a rather intimate household of five, and now he was thrust into an enormous family. Apa and Ama (as Juan called this set of grandparents as well) slept in the big bedroom and three girls took the second bedroom, leaving the boys—nine of them, including Juan—to crowd into the living room.

One can only imagine the challenges that arose when it came to meal times, but Basilia ran a tight ship and fed the family in shifts for breakfast and supper. Come 7 p.m., the kitchen was closed, no exceptions. "No matter if we were still hungry, she would not change her mind, and I don't blame her," Juan said. "Ama was a very loving mother to me and my siblings and she never complained of the number of children in the house, as this was her responsibility of being a mother and grandmother."

The house did have one luxury that Juan wasn't used to. His grandparents owned a small *working* black-and-white television. For the nation, these were the television industry's golden years, filling the evenings with Jack Benny, the *Lone Ranger*, *Bonanza*, *Rin Tin Tin*, and Steve Allen. At the Flores home, however, the set was usually only turned on to watch the nightly news. Still, Juan felt special to be living in a house with such a modern amenity.

It didn't make life after Amelia's death much easier. "I wanted to be loved, and sometimes I felt alone; so I often would go to the city cemetery to have time for myself," Juan recalled. "It was located one block from the house, and to me, it was just a quiet park. I laid next to the headstones and daydreamed about what it would feel like to have had a real mother and father, like many of my friends did. I remember that I prayed to God for a family with a real mom and dad. I often dozed off to sleep for a few minutes. One day, my brother Ray, found me there and gave me a hug. We walked back together to Ama's house. We did not talk about it. He understood that we both missed our mother."

The expenses of such a large household were more manageable when the children pitched in. Juan's uncle Adolph Flores was living at home when Juan and his siblings arrived, and he remembered how that period was a challenge financially, but not that much out of the norm. "There were good time and bad times. My mother took care of anyone who came to live with us. It was what it was," he said. "Without being in the military, it was hard [for people from the West Side] to come by good jobs, but we kids started work early to earn money. A lot of people we knew picked some cotton before the holidays to get by."

There would be another big difference that came with living with the Flores family. This new experience, though, was no luxury like television. Each summer since the early 1940s, Jesus, Basilia, and whichever kids were living at home traveled to Taft in South Texas to pick cotton. For the next six years Juan joined them in the fields.

That first summer, about mid-July 1958, he felt a change come over the household as Ama and Apa began preparing for the trip. Juan, age 10, had never worked a job, much less one that took him so far away from home (a home he was just getting used to living in). Then the day arrived when the adventure truly started. As Juan observed, the quiet of dawn was suddenly shattered by the sound of a big truck honking its horn outside the house. Trini Encino sat inside the truck, bidding the family a good morning. "Don Trini," as Juan learned to call Encino ("Don" being a title of respect), was responsible for picking workers every year and driving them to the cotton fields. As crew leader, Encino always chose Jesus Flores because there were acres and acres of cotton to be picked and he considered the Floreses a good and large cotton-picking family.

So after Encino honked his horn again, Jesus Flores locked his house and joined his family in the back of the truck. It had a long, open bed with boards on both sides, and it carried about 25 people. *El truckero*, as Encino was also called for obvious reasons, picked up other families before turning his truck south and heading toward the Texas Gulf Coast. On the floor of the truck were caches of supplies brought by each family, including pots, utensils, washtubs, and small kerosene stoves for cooking. Basilia also packed a kerosene lamp, blankets, clothes—everything needed for spending the rest of the summer away from home.

"During the drive, I remember feeling the warm wind and the hot Texas sun as it shined brightly on our faces," said Juan. "We had a few bathroom stops at local gas stations or just the bushes, somewhere along that long road. We all knew that we had to go to the back of the facility because we were accustomed to signs all around the areas that read, 'Mexicans go to the back.' None of us questioned the signs because we did not know any different. We were very much aware and accustomed to this because our families told us that was the way of life."

The trip took over six hours, with Juan, his family, and a truckload of strangers enduring the rising heat of the day. When they finally arrived at the camp, near the small town of Taft, Juan saw a number of wooden shacks. One of them would be his family's home for the duration of the summer. It had three separate living quarters, one per family. Inside each shack there was a single room, absolutely empty, with a concrete floor, in which Basilia would spend a lot of time constantly sweeping out the dust from the nearby fields. It had electricity and a single light socket in the middle of the ceiling. There were two windows with hinged wooden flaps that could be propped open with a stick. Although there was no running water inside, everyone used an outdoor spigot to get water for cooking, washing, and drinking. There was also an outside shower stall, where groups of frogs tended to gather.

A travel chest became a table, and large, empty food cans were used for chairs. "Or you just sat on the concrete floor," remembered Juan.

At night, Juan's grandparents slept on the floor using a small matt cushioned with cotton-picking sacks. The girls and some boys made do with their own sacks and any other padding available. (The other boys slept outside, atop their sacks and under the Texas sky.) Everything was picked up in the morning so that the space could be used as a kitchen and dining room throughout the day.

In the early 20th century, as many Mexicans were fleeing their country to escape the atrocities of the Mexican Revolution, others were crossing into Texas for job opportunities. According to the *Handbook of Texas*, "The rapid expansion of Texas agriculture was primarily responsible for the migration of Mexicans from 1900 to 1930." This migration included the thousands who worked the state's many agricultural jobs, including in the cotton fields.[1]

When Juan looked around at the camp, with perhaps 30 to 40 people assembled to work in the fields the next day, all he saw were brown faces. He would remember that scene later in his life, when he learned about slavery in the U.S. and how the slaves worked the southern cotton fields, and when he spoke about picking cotton with other people in different parts of the country. The reality, he discovered, was that people from several races and backgrounds actually kept the cotton industry afloat in the 19th and 20th centuries with their labor. But on that first night, not exactly knowing what was to come the next day, he bedded down on his sack alongside his brothers, uncles and aunts, assuming that Mexicans and Mexican Americans like him were the only ones who picked cotton.

The workday started each morning before sunrise, when Jesus Flores began rousting everyone awake. "I don't know how Apa knew the time of the day because there was no alarm clock, but he knew," said Juan. The kids washed their faces, bodies, and hands in the washtub at the side of the house, then donned long-sleeve shirts and hats for protection from the sun and biting insects, especially mosquitoes. (There was no sunscreen or insect repellent.)

Basilia spent her dawns cooking. Breakfast usually consisted of flour tortillas, Spam, and cheese. She also prepared lunch, which was the same as breakfast, wrapped in cloth to take to the fields in a tin bucket.

Besides feeding her small army of workers, Basilia ensured that the heavy canvas sacks used to carry the cotton were in usable condition. Because these sacks were dragged on the ground during the harvest, they were frequently plagued with small rips and large tears. In addition to patching the sacks, she mended clothes that needed to last until fall.

Not long after finishing breakfast, Juan heard the horn of Encino's truck and climbed with his family into the back with the rest of the pickers. Encino drove his crew to a nearby farm with fields ready for harvesting. Once there, Jesus Flores gathered his family around him to give instructions and assignments as to which rows to pick. After checking everyone's sacks, and with the sun still low in the sky, he'd send them into the fields to do *la pisca*, the picking.

When Juan turned to the cotton field, becoming more visible with each passing moment of the early morning, it didn't seem real. "When I first saw the rows of cotton, they seemed like they would never end. The end seemed very far away—like two or three city blocks long," he said. It would take forever, the young boy stood thinking, to get to the far end of the row. He didn't yet realize that—even if he did somehow manage to get there—he'd just have to turn around, get to the next row over, and begin again.

"We immediately got into our 'hunchback' positions, stooping over the plants, picking at the cotton bolls with our bare hands, which was very difficult at first because the plants are wrapped with thick prickly dried leaves, and we got stuck often and our hands bled," said Juan, who, 60 years later, still recalled how it felt to reach down and pick those first handfuls of cotton. "It took about a week for our hands to get toughened and develop calluses, but then they didn't bleed anymore."

Juan's uncle Adolph Flores had put in a lot of time in the fields long before Juan arrived on the scene and was pragmatic about the work. "I was born on a farm in Branchville in 1929," he said. "My father was a sharecropper. I would feed the chickens, milk the cows. My father had a good work ethic, and he taught us about working hard. And cotton-picking was hard work, but that's just what you had to do."

Each picker's long pick sack was slung low from the shoulder, dragging through the dirt between the rows, so that both hands could retrieve the puffy white bolls of cotton, the stickers too, and then stuff them quickly away. An adult sack measured up to 12 feet long, while the children carried shorter sacks. Although some crew leaders were instructed by the farmer to have their workers pick only the soft, white cotton off the plant, Encino told Jesus Flores that he wanted the whole boll pulled to get as much cotton as possible. Everyone worked at their best pace, filling their sacks as quickly as possible, and regardless of whether picked or pulled, each handful of cotton added just a little bit more weight to their burden.

Cotton harvesting was backbreaking work because pickers needed to bend over to reach the plants. When that position got to be too much to take, they'd continue on their hands and knees. Everyone worked their way toward Encino's cotton trailer, parked at the end of the long rows. It seemed like it took forever to fill his sack, but when it was full (or too heavy to drag much further), Juan took it to a set of scales on a sturdy wooden tripod next to the trailer, where the cotton was weighed. Encino credited Jesus Flores for each family member's cotton. When it was full, the trailer of cotton was taken to the gin, located about three miles away, for processing.

After emptying his sack, Juan usually took a few moments to sit in the shade, rest, and get a drink of water. Everyone was paid by the pound, not by the hour; so, too soon, Jesus Flores would stand tall among the rows and yell for Juan to get back to work. Once in the fields again, stooped over and working, Juan heard Apa shout, *"Sume la bota!"* which translates as "Step on the boot!" and was his way of saying "Give it the best you can." It was a rallying cry of motivation, one that would stay with Juan his entire life. Whenever he felt like he was near the end of his energy or at a loss of spirit, he would hear his grandfather's words and find the strength of will to continue.

"I remember that hearing those words would always encourage us to continue picking even though we were tired," Juan said. He had quickly realized that cotton equaled money, and the family's survival through the winter meant 10-hour days in the summer with as many hands on the harvest as possible. He tried very hard to keep up, but it was challenging work. "It was hard picking cotton. The sun was so hot that it made me dizzy, and sometimes it dazed me. It felt like time stopped. One could get weighted down with fatigue due to the growing heaviness of the cotton sack."

Since Juan was younger and new at the task, his grandfather paid special attention to him so that he wouldn't fall too far behind or get heat exhaustion. On his knees, wearing kneepads, Apa sometimes picked two rows at a time, his and Juan's. He'd pull the cotton and leave it for Juan to put in his sack. On occasion, Juan was told to fetch some water, and he'd return carrying a large jug of water, walking down the rows to let his family drink from a tin can.

Standing in the fields, a blazing sun overhead, his weary brothers stopping their work just long enough to stretch tall their backs and gulp down some water, Juan had had too little experience in this world to imagine that someday some of the most important voices in the halls of Congress would tell his story—this story—of picking cotton with his family. This, they would say, was surely where his dedication to hard work, not to mention his loyalty to family, truly began. But at that moment, pouring another drink for his exhausted family members, knowing that there were hours of work left in the day before dinner, Juan was simply trying his best to prove himself and be a vital worker.

After a couple weeks in the fields, Juan was getting used to the routine and pretty much used to the searing heat of the afternoons. He was about as familiar with the bugs—some as big as his thumb—that lived in the plants. When he found a steady rhythm with his hands, he'd often lose himself to daydreams.

"There was one specific time of seeing cars drive by in the distance on the small country road. I could only imagine how it was to be driving that car and not be in the field," Juan recalled of an afternoon long ago. The sound of automobiles always pulled his attention away from his work. He tried to guess where they came from and where they were headed. "I also remember when a convertible passed by and the couple was smiling and enjoying themselves and listening to the music on the radio as the air touched their faces."

One could not afford to daydream too long, for the fields held some danger. In addition to the possibility of suffering from the heat, there was a very real threat of running into rattlesnakes sleeping in the lower husks of the plants or sunning themselves in the middle of the rows. Pickers tended to work in groups to avoid surprising them.

When it came time to weigh the cotton, there was an additional physical endeavor for Juan to pull off: slinging the full sack of cotton over his shoulder, climbing the wooden ladder on the side of the trailer, and emptying the sack into the bed. All this when he was at his most exhausted and sore; it sometimes led to mishaps.

"When I was 13 years old, I climbed up the ladder and—I may have been almost at the top, I really don't remember—I fell off. Anyway, every cotton picker knew to take the strap from around your neck and fold it between your shoulder and the sack. On this particular day, for some reason or other, I did not do so and as I scrambled up the ladder, the sack fell off my shoulder and, due to its weight, snapped my neck and pulled me to the ground. When I hit the ground, I hit hard. I was definitely dazed and disoriented. Don Trini was standing by the scales and saw me land on the ground, and he quickly rushed to check on me. Although I was in pain—and luckily the sack didn't break my neck—I felt more embarrassed than anything else. Believe me, I never made that mistake again."

Sore pride, sore hands, sore back—none of that mattered. At the end of the day, it all came down to the amount of cotton a person picked. Some had fast hands and strong backs and could pick hundreds of pounds a day.

"My grandpa was a very decent cotton-picker," said José Vasquez Jr. "On a good day he could pick over 500 pounds, even though he was getting up in age."

"Sometimes, the fields were beautiful with a lot of cotton, sometimes the drought left them looking pretty bad," said Adolph Flores. "I could pick 500 to 800 pounds when I was really working hard and if the fields were full."

Of course, not every picker could bring in that kind of haul, but with the number of workers in his family, Jesus Flores could make a reasonable amount of money. And because of their need to earn as much as possible for the coming year, the Flores family couldn't afford to leave any white puffs unpicked. Besides, Jesus Flores always wanted his family to be the best by harvesting the most cotton. Juan understood that by being the "best" in the camp, it brought respect to the family. That made everyone work harder: *Sume la bota!*

After a dinner of carne asada, rice, and beans, Juan and the rest of the family slept like rocks. As Juan remembered, it didn't matter if they weren't sleeping inside the shack. "After a hard day's work, we were too tired to know the difference," he said of his nights spent beneath a blanket of stars.

But things changed on Friday when, even after such exhaustive work, the camp took on a lighter feeling. Two days without work lie ahead. "At the end of the week, your back hurt, but to me the weekends were a lot of fun," said José Jr.

If Fridays were a day of expectant happiness in the camps, Saturdays were positively celebratory. In Manuel Peña's memoir *Where the Ox Does Not Plow: A Mexican American Ballad*, he writes tenderly about growing up in Texas as a member of a migrant cotton-picking family, with similar trials and tribulations as the Flores family. Peña also recalls the particular lightness of Saturdays. "For youngsters like my brother Plon and me, Saturday was a magical day. *Sábado de Gloria*, the Mexican workers called it, literally, 'Saturday of glory'."

For one thing, it was payday. On Saturday mornings, Encino paid cash for the amount of cotton Jesus Flores and his family harvested that week, usually between $250 and $300. Jesus would always called over his grandson Juan. "Apa would ask me to double check the amount of money that we were paid," said Juan. "He would call me to his side and say, *"Mijo, cuentalo el dinero. Es correcto?"* ("Son, count the money. Is it correct?")

Then Jesus Flores paid his family members for their work. "I remember my first pay day, as most people do, I think," said Juan. "Based on the amount of cotton I picked, I earned $2 cash for the week, and that was a lot for me!" It was good pay for a 10-year old boy, who stood about 4-feet tall and weighed 90 pounds (if his belly was full). As Juan got older and bigger and learned the skills better, he would more than double that weekly income. At the end of his tenure in the cotton fields, when he was 15, he stood five-feet tall, weighed about 100 pounds, and was regularly earning $45 a week, picking and earning as much as Apa.

On Saturdays, Encino also drove some of his crew about 19 miles to Corpus Christi to shop for the week. Jesus and Basilia always went, and they usually took Juan with them so that he could read the prices in English at the supermarket. As Juan helped Ama buy dry goods, potatoes, beans, flour, and Spam, Apa waited outside the store with the rest of the men. Afterward, they all might have a fried chicken lunch, and before leaving town Juan would want to visit the Kress department store to buy a lime soda and a banana split with some of his newly earned wages.

On typical Saturdays, everyone wore their "Sunday best" clothes to Corpus Christi because there wasn't much to do but rest in the camp all day Sunday. That wasn't good enough for Juan and some of the other boys. They'd set off on foot toward the Gulf of Mexico, about 10 miles away, hoping to spend a day at the beach, playing in the waves. But after walking several miles they'd always settle for swimming in the closer and calmer waters of Nueces Bay at Portland, near Corpus Cristi. Still, that water was a cooling balm, and their time away from the fields was a restorative period they had to themselves before walking back to camp, where work would always come bright and early the next morning.

Some Tuesday evenings after work Encino drove some families to Taft, about five miles away, where, as Juan remembered it, there was "The friendliest cotton-pickin' town in Texas" painted on a large commercial building. In Taft, Ama and Apa could buy supplies such as kerosene, and hoes to pull the weeds that surrounded the cotton plants. They occasionally needed new cotton sacks to replace the ones that had suffered holes too large even for Basilia to repair.

Because of the geographic enormity of Texas, the cotton crop was always in different growth phases throughout the state. The harvest around Brownsville, Kingsville, and Taft began in late July or early August. After those crops were harvested, many workers and families followed the harvest cycle north to Waxahachie or maybe Burleson, and then on toward the Panhandle to pick the fields around Lubbock and Amarillo. Some workers kept going straight into New Mexico and Oklahoma to pick more cotton before returning to their homes for the winter.

"Each September, on the way north, my grandfather told us boys, '*Los que quieren ir a la escuela, se quedan en San Antonio, y los demas se vienen conmigo.*' (Those of you who want to go to school will stay in San Antonio, and the rest of you will come with me)," Juan said.

Encino dropped off Basilia, along with cousin Loy, Johnny, and Juan to attend school. The rest went with their father to pick more cotton, usually near Hobbs, New Mexico, and when they returned—just in time for Christmas—they had enough money to sustain the family until the summer arrived and the routine started again.

In 1963, the cotton crop near Taft was bad enough that, after spending little time harvesting there, Encino drove the family to Waxahachie to work. Even though Jesus Flores was still considered a good picker, at age 68 he was beginning to slow down. His body was still strong, but the aches in his back and his knees went deeper and lasted longer. He couldn't count the number of miles he had traveled in his lifetime looking for work nor even guess how many tons of cotton he had harvested. But Social Security withholdings had been made mandatory only a few years earlier, and now he could begin receiving retirement funds. That surely influenced his plan to quit the cotton-picking business for good.

"The rule of thumb for the family had always been that children and grandchildren picked cotton until he or she married and moved away," Juan explained. "But that year Apa made us a deal: If we each got a job, we wouldn't need to pick cotton the following summer. We took the deal."

It had been a tough way to spend his summers, Juan would later admit, but those months helped him form a solid bond with his family and, as he came of age, helped instill a sense of pride in his hard work. Picking cotton tested him physically and sometimes set his mind adrift, yet, those annual endeavors would always be well remembered and cherished. "It was kind of sad because it was a way of life really coming to an end," he said, referring not just to a steady revenue stream for the Flores family but also for the kind of work they had been doing. "I did not comprehend fully how machines would replace us pickers but Apa knew. Apa had seen these machines in the nearby fields. Within a few years after we left those fields, machines had replaced thousands of Mexican American pickers."

CHAPTER FOUR

Early Education, Witness to History

While summers were spent in the cotton fields, come autumn, it was schooltime for Juan. As a child and teenager, his schooling was in most ways quite typical, while still being unique to his own experiences. Away from any classroom, he learned valuable lessons about life: While very young, for instance, he realized being clever at the bars with Apa Vasquez brought rewards in the form of sodas, chips, and the hearty laughter of adults. He'd also learned how to work hard—very hard—and labor as part of a team in the cotton fields with his extended Flores family. Like any other kid, as he grew older and spent time with friends in the neighborhood, he developed his own views and opinions on right and wrong, and his own likes and dislikes, some of which would stay with him for the rest of his life.

It was in school, though, where he first learned the lesson that speaking Spanish was not allowed in the San Antonio public schools. Until 1973, a Texas Department of Education rule meant that only English could be spoken in the classrooms, in the hallways, in the cafeteria, and even on the playground—by both students and teachers.[1] It was a hard lesson to learn for "John," as Juan was called throughout elementary school. All the students of Mexican descent had their names taken from them, Anglicized, and returned with strict instructions to use only these new names at school.

Although Juan had spoken some English since he was a toddler, he struggled with his studies. While living with his mother, his teachers at José Navarro Elementary School held him back in the second grade for not having a better understanding of English. Of course, with a sick mother and absentee father, he had a lot of emotional issues to contend with in addition to keeping up academic issues. Eventually, he made it to third grade.

After Amelia Vasquez died in 1957, Jesus and Basilia Flores took in and eventually adopted their daughter's four kids and took full responsibility for their welfare, including their schooling. After starting the third grade at James Fannin Elementary, Juan appeared to have a stable enough home life to begin making his way up the academic ladder with surer footing. He made it through the sixth grade without much incident or fanfare. He followed that with three years at Edgar Allan Poe Junior High School, which were not especially remarkable either. Although schoolwork had become easier because he could speak and understand English better, there was not much in his classrooms to hold his interest. He liked numbers a little bit, and sometimes math class could raise his curiosity, but mostly he daydreamed about being far away from school, playing basketball or football with his friends—on really boring days, even picking cotton appealed more than school did.

With no real thought to the future, Juan enrolled at Louis W. Fox Vocational and Technical High School downtown, about 10 miles from his home; it had a large Mexican American population and was known throughout San Antonio as "Fox Tech" or just "Tech." (Fox Tech essentially had developed directly from the city's first public high school, originally named Central Grammar and High School, established in 1879.[2])

"This was the kind of school one attends to learn a trade, for example, how to fix a car or television, or how to become a beautician or a secretary," Juan said. "Although this is an oversimplification, it didn't seem that it was for anyone interested in academics or who wanted to go to college."

After catching two city buses he arrived for his first day at Tech extremely tired—wiped out, in fact. At least he wasn't expected to begin classwork right away. This was orientation day, and like everyone else he was instructed to pick a trade or shop subject in order to assign him the right classes that would complement his academic schedule. Juan thought he might want to be an auto mechanic; so he signed up for that track as his first choice. The counselor also needed Juan to make a second selection "just in case." After thinking for a while and remembering that a friend of a relative worked as a radio and television repairman and seemed to make good money, Juan signed up for those courses as a backup.

Whether Juan would have made a good auto mechanic will never be known because he was assigned his second choice. He wasn't told (or perhaps he was too sleepy to have clearly understood) that he would have to follow this vocational track, half of each school day, for the rest of his high school years. It would hardly matter what he was assigned, though, because by his own admission, Juan never exerted himself too hard, whether in his academic or vocational classes. He often found himself quite tired in the classroom.

There were reasons—not excuses—for his mind to be too sleepy to pay much attention. His first day at Tech, in fact, just happened to follow his first day of a new job. Actually, it was his first night of a new job.

Back in the autumn of 1963, when Jesus Flores promised that any kid who found a job didn't have to pick cotton anymore, Juan started working at the San Antonio Dental Laboratory, delivering dentures and other dental work to the various downtown dentist offices for $17.50 a week, plus

33 cents an hour extra for working half-days on Saturdays. He could walk to most of these offices, but if his destination was too far away, he took the bus. In between deliveries, Juan often noticed some teenagers hanging around a concession stand located outside the lab's building. After several days, Juan introduced himself to one of them, a boy named Bobby. They talked about their jobs and Juan found out that Bobby was a bicycle messenger for Western Union Telegraph Company. Bobby made his job sound like easy work, and he was paid $1.25 an hour.

Juan did the math and realized he could be making more money with Western Union, and so he quickly applied for a position at the office, located a couple blocks away from the dental lab. He was hired. "My first day on the job was the night before I started high school," said Juan, adding that, to his surprise at the time, piloting a one-speed bicycle with fat tires for hours on end was not the easy task that Bobby had said it was. "I learned very fast that I was not physically in shape to ride for eight hours a shift. The roundtrips to the San Antonio Airport were about two-hour rides."

It turned out that not only was this job a lot harder than walking a box of dentures down the block, Juan had been hired for the 3pm to 11pm shift. That first night he was sent out to deliver a telegram to a destination north of Loop 410, about ten miles away from the Western Union office. Returning from that delivery on a bike with no headlight, he found himself pursued by what sounded like a hundred barking dogs snapping at the pedals. "I picked up my feet and placed them on the handlebars," Juan said. "I was on top of a hill and sped down fast, the wind blowing on my face and hair. I was glad that the dogs stopped chasing me!"

As if that episode wasn't enough, he also got caught in the rain that night. At one point, his leg muscles were so sore that he suddenly stopped his bike and collapsed with exhaustion on the grass next to the street. "I was so angry with myself that I cried because I was behind schedule and I knew I could not let Apa down," he said, expressing his desire as a young man to impress his grandfather Flores, who had always urged him to try his hardest, no matter what job he was doing. "I was determined to meet my commitment because I did not want to go back to the cotton fields. I was glad that it was dark so that nobody could see me cry. I prayed to God to give me the strength to go on. I finally found my composure and got my strength to complete work."

Arriving back at the office around 1:30 am, Juan felt like quitting on the spot if the night dispatcher, known as "Popp," snapped at him. Although Popp had a terrible reputation for intimidating the bicycle messengers, he just stared for a while at his new young charge before quietly clocking him out for the night. Juan bicycled back to his house and collapsed on his bed, still wearing his dirty clothes.

"The next morning was the first day of high school," Juan said, "and I don't remember much about it because I think I slept through it."

In the early 1950s, Leonard Krzywosinski started as a clerk at the Western Union counter, taking in telegrams and money orders for $25 a week. After about ten years he was transferred to the delivery department as a dispatcher, where he sent out messengers with telegrams. "The job was something that I liked," said Krzywosinski, many decades later. (He worked for Western Union for 41 years, ending his career as office manager.) "You never knew when something might happen. That's why we were open all night."

Once the messengers experienced a few tough shifts, it could be hard keeping enough boys on staff. "We were doing more than just looking for bodies that could bicycle a lot," explained Krzywosinski. "I was looking for a bit of education, responsibility, and being dependable." He remembers working with Juan (Krzywosinski called him "John") because it was unusual for messengers to stay as long as he did. "We had so many coming and going. In the messenger department, no one really stayed a long time. For most of them, it was a job that they might quit when they found something better or easier. John stayed a long time. We could depend on him."

That included working during the especially busy occasions, like Mother's Day, Valentine's Day, and Easter. Western Union's Candygrams included a box of chocolates with a telegram and became wildly popular gifts. On those days, remembered Juan, "Each eight-hour shift was physically a killer."

In the mid–20th century, one of the fastest ways for reporters to deliver news was through the use of teletype machines, which were owned and operated by Western Union. At that time, Western Union had contracts with the Associated Press (AP) and United Press International (UPI) allowing reporters to send their news stories over these machines.[3] At the site where the news happened, a designated typist would input the reporter's stories into the teletype machine. The information was sent across the country to other machines, which printed it onto paper. The local dispatcher at the Western Union office determined whether the information was to be delivered or discarded.

On the afternoon of June 6, 1966, Juan was waiting in the office to be dispatched. It seemed like any other day until he saw the dispatcher, an older Caucasian gentleman, standing behind the counter, separating the telegrams. "I saw him looking at a teletype page and then say, 'How dare him?' and 'Good.' " Juan didn't know what the dispatcher was referring to, but his boss used an ethnic slur before throwing the page in the trash can.

As he was a teenager, curiosity got its fingers into Juan's imagination. He had a "gut feeling" that the paper was something important. When the dispatcher walked outside the building to smoke, Juan casually strolled to the trashcan, looked around in all directions, and then bent over and took hold of the discarded pages. On a hunch, he stamped the paper with the date and time using the Western Union time clock and quickly stuffed it in his pocket. He felt scared. If the dispatcher saw him taking teletypes out of the trash, he knew he'd be fired.

But he also was angry and upset. His working-class neighborhood was predominantly African American, and some of the boys had become his friends—playing games together, football and basketball, going to the movies, swimming. His neighbors were good citizens, just like his family; so he felt very uncomfortable whenever someone like the Western Union dispatcher used the ethnic slur that he'd uttered before wadding up the teletype paper and throwing it away.

When Juan's shift was over, after leaving the office, Juan read the discarded teletype-telegram:

> "James H. Meredith, who set out to show Mississippi Negroes they had nothing to fear, was killed from ambush today as he walked along a Mississippi Highway... Meredith—the Negro student who cracked the racial barrier at the University of Mississippi in 1962—was on the second day of the March."[4]

Meredith was walking from Memphis, Tennessee, to Jackson, Mississippi, to rally African Americans to vote during a very turbulent time in what was a very turbulent decade. In the teletype, Meredith was quoted as saying before the march, "First, we want to tear down the fear that grips Negroes in Mississippi, and we want to encourage the 450,000 Negroes remaining unregistered (as voters) in Mississippi."

The news of Meredith's death shook Juan. It was terrible. It was horrific. It had gone out all over the country. And it was wrong: although Meredith was shot several times at close range with a shotgun, he lived through the murder attempt. (*Life* magazine published photos of Meredith struggling by the roadside seconds after getting shot.)[5] As Juan kept reading, he finally saw that another telegram had been issued correcting the record.

After news of the shooting spread around the country, though, some high-profile civil rights advocates, including Stokely Carmichael and Martin Luther King Jr., took up the march, vowing to complete it in Meredith's name. When the marchers arrived in Jackson, Meredith was walking with them.[6]

Having never spoken to his dispatcher about these news items or why he'd decided they were only worthy of the trash, Juan decided to hold onto the pages. For him, they would become reminders of what people of color in this country went through in their struggle to have their civil rights recognized.

While businesses and many professionals were used to receiving telegrams, not every family looked forward to the Western Union messenger knocking on their door—certainly not since the military action in Vietnam was ramping up. Since San Antonio traditionally boasted a healthy military volunteer rate, families with sons and daughters in the armed forces dreaded the thought of receiving a telegram from the Department of Defense.

One day, Juan was assigned to deliver a "debt notice," which typically came from utilities companies and required the addressee be confirmed first so that the telegram could be left under the door if nobody was home. Juan had just tried unsuccessfully to confirm the address at the house next door to where the telegram was supposed to be delivered when the woman who lived there came home. She saw Juan walking away from her house with a telegram in his hand and a yellow plastic Western Union badge clipped to his shirt. She started yelling and screaming because she thought the telegram was for her. The woman's husband appeared immediately to see the commotion and Juan had to quickly explain the situation. After helping his wife recover, the man apologized, saying that they had a son in Vietnam. This first time encountering a parent who was sure that their son had died stunned Juan; he could only stand on the sidewalk for a few moments in silence before dropping off the telegram at the correct house and then quickly leaving.

If the emotions in Juan's heart were sent into a tailspin on a simple misunderstanding of a debt notice, they were almost uncontrollable when he actually had to deliver telegrams announcing soldiers' deaths. *Almost* because he had already known death, though he was too young when his mother died to truly comprehend what death really meant. Now, he was growing as a young man while learning something about the concept through others' pain. Possessing this unique perspective, he found himself becoming more interested in the mysterious fight going on in Vietnam, where all those other young men named in those telegrams had lost their lives. (In later years of the war, the Department of Defense directly took over informing the families of injured or killed soldiers.)

His Western Union job took him to places and events that other people in his life, his school, and his neighborhood would never dream of finding themselves. Such as it was when Juan worked alongside the White House press corps in early March 1966. While President Lyndon Johnson visited his Texas ranch, about 60 miles north of San Antonio, Juan had been assigned to the Tropicano Motor Hotel, where national and local reporters received briefings of the first family's activities.[7] Juan's job was to walk the reporters' written copy over to the Western Union attendant, a few blocks away, who then sent it to the typist.

Later that same year, on Christmas Eve, President Johnson visited Kelly Air Force Base in San Antonio,[8] and Juan was dispatched to that location as well. For this occasion, the president and his wife, Claudia "Lady Bird" Johnson, were on hand to welcome home wounded soldiers from Vietnam. The day was crisp and sunny but with a few clouds, when the C-131 landed and taxied to a stop. Soldiers in dress uniform stood at attention on one side of the plane while anxious families waited with tears and smiles on the other side. Juan was stationed in a nearby hangar, where he could see the soldiers being brought out of the plane on stretchers and down a ramp. Some of them still had IV lines in their arms. At the bottom of the ramp stood the Johnsons, bending over to greet each wounded soldier and shaking his hand if possible. At one point, an overjoyed mother or wife cut in front of the president to give a returning soldier a kiss. Johnson looked delighted at her boldness.

The soldiers were then transferred by ambulance to the army hospital at Fort Sam Houston. After Juan returned to the Western Union office, where telegrams were coming in for the wounded soldiers, he was dispatched to the army hospital. Even though he had just been standing within a hundred or so yards of the President of the United States, he found himself much more moved by what he found there. "The first thing that I noticed when I entered the hospital was the strong smell of medicine," Juan said. "Many soldiers were completely covered in white cloth. They had suffered terrible burns. There were also many soldiers with broken bones, and their arms and legs were set in casts, and stretched and supported on poles. When I saw those soldiers, I felt speechless and scared. It was an eerie feeling. It brought home the reality of the war."

Away from his high school classrooms, Juan was getting an education on the real consequences of the war overseas while increasingly becoming aware of how his country was also at war with itself over civil rights. Perhaps just as importantly, he had seen so much of his own hometown by traveling along so many different streets and visiting hundreds of businesses and homes. He'd seen firsthand how others lived in the segregated neighborhoods of San Antonio, and he began to really comprehend how the city had been deficient in its treatment of people like him—Mexican Americans.

Being hit on the hands with a ruler in school for speaking Spanish, having to use the back sides of businesses—he'd been told these were simply "the way things were" over and over when he was a kid. And he'd never really questioned it. "That was the way of life," Juan said, pointing out that some things seemed to balance out in his head when he was young. "When we went to the movies and sat in the balcony for cheaper than all the kids below us, I didn't notice any difference, nor did I care. I just looked around and smiled that we were at the movies. We were all looking at the same movie!"

But then he'd started delivering telegrams throughout the city. "When I worked as a messenger, I noticed the discrimination. I realized the differences in the city economically." For instance, one time he delivered a telegram to a school located in the much more affluent north side of San Antonio, and he saw its beautiful facilities and its gymnasium with nicely painted metal lockers and clean new benches. "I couldn't believe how nice it looked in contrast to our gym at Fox Tech," Juan said. "Ours was nicely kept but we had old wooden lockers. I'm pretty sure they were discolored. They were not exactly run down, but I didn't know how old they looked until I saw the beautiful ones at that other school. That's when I realized how different things were."

He was growing up and growing a bit wiser, but the lessons learned during this early education period of his life weren't necessarily translating to success in the classroom. He continued struggling with his hands-on vocational track and wasn't much better with academics as he began to think about life after graduation.

That is, *if* he graduated. It's fair to say that because he exerted more effort and determination at his job than at school, he was very close to not moving on to senior year with his classmates.

"I remember very well that, one day, my radio and TV teacher told me if I promised not to return to his class he would give me a D-," said Juan, who believed his teacher understood he had no interest in the subject. "Of course, I agreed, and so I was passed to the twelfth grade!"

Being a senior didn't much improve Juan's ambitions toward radio and TV repair. He was a working man already and did the best he could in school, whenever he had the energy. As the year passed, he noticed that his friends were getting excited about graduation for their various reasons, but at the same time there was a growing tension in the hallways "because the Vietnam War was just getting bigger and more dangerous," Juan remembered. "Many of my friends were getting ready to go and fight. We had heard stories of some of our students coming back in body bags, and this was quite alarming. But I, too, thought about enlisting after I graduated."

In fact, while in high school, a soldier was the first thing Juan had ever really given much thought to becoming. This, after his unique experiences as a messenger. This, after seeing wounded soldiers who couldn't raise their arms to shake the president's hand. This, after seeing those soldiers, burned and broken, in the hospital. This, after hearing the stories of the body bags. But he'd also heard that being in the military gave a person a good career path. He'd had an uncle who was a sergeant in the Air Force and always talked about the benefits and the travel and how he was happy raising his family while in the service. Patriotism was running high throughout San Antonio. It seemed like nearly every neighborhood he delivered telegrams to had houses with American flags in the windows or hung from the porches, and he knew that meant a son (or two or more) was away fighting in Vietnam. Several of his cousins had joined up already. It was easy to get swept up in the spirit of volunteerism.

One day, Juan walked into an enlistment station. "As I sat there, I saw many boys who had been drafted. They all were talking about going to the war to kill 'Charlie', as the Viet Cong soldiers were often called by American troops. I was kind of scared of what they were saying," Juan admitted. "I got to talking to some of the boys in the room, and they asked me if I was drafted, and I said I was volunteering. They told me that I was crazy, so I left in a hurry. I decided to wait until I graduated to complete this process."

That is, *if* he graduated.

CHAPTER FIVE

When Juan Met Terry

When the spotlight hit Juan Vasquez's portrait within the *American Dream* mural at Mi Tierra, everyone applauded and then turned to acknowledge the man himself. Juan waved quickly, smiling from ear to ear, though still humbly. Sitting next to him, Terry felt "tears of joy and accomplishment" welling up when they looked into each other's eyes.

"Once upon a time, a few years ago, Juan and I were having breakfast at Mi Tierra when one of the owners, Jorge Cortez, came by our table to say hi," said Terry. "On an impulse, I asked if they had ever considered Juan for the wall. He smiled and said they were in the process of putting him on the mural wall but were waiting for a picture to be sent from [Juan and Terry's oldest son] Juan Jr. I smiled and said, 'Jorge, I will email it to you ASAP.'"

It was a typical response from Terry, who was not just Juan's wife but also his long-time advocate and font of support. Which is why, on the day of Juan's ceremony for the mural, those who knew something of Juan's life story were applauding for both him and Terry. "I felt super excited. Thrilled," said Terry. "I just remembered how far we had come together."

Twelfth grade at Fox Tech was going to be different for Juan. The previous school years had included some challenging academic times, but with continued stability with his home life (in other words, he wasn't moving from house to house anymore), and with a little good fortune he was destined to find something that truly mattered toward his future, something that would bring him more than just some success in the classroom.

He'd already demonstrated critical thinking toward the future by using his wages earned from being a bicycle messenger to buy a car, a 1953 four-door Chevrolet Bel Air from his cousin Loy for $150 cash, (before Loy left for the navy in summer 1966). It was beautiful, too, with a white top, baby blue body, and just enough chrome to keep the whole thing shining in the abundant Texas sunshine. Juan was promoted to car messenger at Western Union, meaning he could deliver his telegrams much faster without having to blast his thighs and calves through dog-infested streets on his bike anymore.

Despite owning a car, he still took two buses to high school, where there was limited student parking. At the beginning of senior year, his enthusiasm for academics hadn't changed much, but he was a little more excited about going to school because, as a junior, he'd become active in the Tech Little Theatre, the school's performing arts department. Juan was part of the production crew that helped produce the plays. Being in this extracurricular activity proved satisfying for Juan, who was growing up very sociable and good-natured with a healthy sense of humor. Juan said, "Being in the production crew, and even playing some small parts on stage, gave me the opportunity to meet other people."

When senior year began, Juan enthusiastically continued working with the props department, which met regularly after school. A fellow senior, Georgina Cardenas (then Georgina Vasquez, no relation), also put in long hours to prepare for three productions that year, *Party Line, Get Witch Quick*, and *Annie Get Your Gun*. "We were there, a lot. A good six hours a day, every day," said Cardenas. "Our theater director Mrs. [Elaine] Curran was director of the Music Theater of San Antonio. We had access to a lot of props and materials, but we still had to go to Sears and other places nearby to buy specific items. We had to paint props and get things to the sewing department. And we'd rehearse with the cast when it got closer to the production."

Crew members often played extras and small roles during the shows, and Juan had played a bit part his junior year in *The King and I*; in his senior year he continued appearing on stage, including as the character Milo for *Get Witch Quick*. In the senior musical, *Annie Get Your Gun*, some songs required Juan, Georgina, and their friend Janie Hernandez to be on stage in costume with everyone else. The only exception was the prop crew wasn't supposed to sing. "We were told to just move our lips," said Cardenas. "But sometimes we'd get carried away. In rehearsals, Mrs. Curran would be in the back of the theater saying, 'Stop singing Janie, Juan, and Georgina!' "

Cardenas also remembered that, for late-night set building and prop coordinating, the crew had to get their own dinners. "I remember Juan was very good at figuring out how much money was needed. And we would hit him up for a nickel or dime, and he was always very nice. If he had it, he would give it," she said.

Having spent so much time with Juan that school year, Cardenas recalled him as "very hard working, and funny, too. He was always thinking. We'd be trying to decide how to do something for a show, trying to solve some problem, and he always looked to be listening to everyone, really paying attention to what they were saying."

In addition to being the theater director, Curran also taught speech class, and part of her curriculum included students performing a play. Curran asked Juan (who was not in her class) to help with the play, and he happily agreed.

During rehearsals, Juan found himself staring at a young woman on stage—it was the woman he would marry one day and who would walk with him nearly every step for the rest of his journey. With her help and encouragement Juan would find success and then build upon it to unimaginable achievements. She would shoulder her own load, too, even taking the lead financially, when necessary. Together, they would carve out a life of happiness and fulfillment. And she was *right there*—standing on the stage in front of him. That day, neither one of them could have dreamed of the life they would share, but still, while preparing to help with the play *Somewhere Over the Rainbow*, it's fair to say Juan quickly found himself over the moon for the lead actress.

"I was instantly inspired the first time I saw her in the theater," he summed up that moment. "I had the opportunity to see her practice every day. I was so impressed with her talent."

He knew her name was Terry Schultz, she was a senior, and she was playing Judy Garland in the show. Juan thought she was quite poised on stage as well as beautiful, and soon enough it hit him: he should ask her out on a date. Without knowing it, Juan had made the best decision of his life, but that didn't make it any easier to carry through with his intentions. She certainly didn't seem to notice him staring at her while she delivered her lines on stage.

After the show ended, he didn't want his chances to slip away. "I remember approaching her for a date, but I was rejected," Juan said. "She told me that she was not dating anyone."

Both of Terry Schultz's parents, Reyes G. Schultz and Mary Ruth Montes, had been born in San Antonio; they were married in April 1938 and soon began a family. After Rosario, Carol, Sylvia, Ray Jr., and Robert came baby Terry. The Schultzes might have assumed that their sixth child was going to be a boy; at least it's pretty clear that they weren't prepared to name the new addition because her birth certificate simply states "baby girl" as her name. Apparently, it took about two months before they settled on Mary Theresa, calling her Terry.

Following Terry, the family kept growing with Mary Guadalupe, Elizabeth, and Ray Anthony. (One baby was lost in childbirth.) Although Reyes and Mary Schultz originally lived in a very small house in the southwest part of town, as their family increased they moved to the West Side neighborhood of Prospect Hill and to a larger, two-story home with a patio and garage.

Mary raised the family. "She was a humble, loving homemaker," Terry remembered. "She'd had some formal education but didn't graduate from high school. She did the best she could to raise her large family, even as we kept growing. My parents also helped raise four grandchildren: Don, Debbie, Doreen, and Louis."

To support his family, Reyes Schultz had held several jobs, including co-owning a gas station with his brother-in-law Jesse Olivarri, before enlisting in the navy. He was stationed at Pearl Harbor after the bombing that brought the country into World War II, and following his service he returned to San Antonio and took a civil service job at Lackland Air Force Base.

Civil service jobs were coveted in San Antonio, and because Reyes was fortunate to get one, Terry was growing up in middle-class surroundings, with real hopes and opportunities for pursuing the American Dream. Life remained relatively simple, without many extras or extravagances, like trips downtown to see movies or variety shows, although on occasion the family vacationed together. "Dad drove us all on an annual summer vacation to Corpus Christi and rented a small beach house. But in a large family you usually just sort of go with the flow. With nine kids our entertainment was usually the neighborhood itself," she said. "I guess the only other entertainment we had was that my mom and dad belonged to a social club, named Club Social Anniversary. It wasn't the big-money type social club; it was a civic organization. The club held charity fundraisers, like dances and pageants." When she was 16, Terry was selected to represent the club in several pageants, including the Miss Latin American pageant and the Fiesta Patrias. The experience of being in the public eye for these events would help her become very sociable in school and throughout her life.

Although in her younger years Terry and her siblings attended Catholic school at Immaculate Heart of Mary, located downtown, later to make financial ends meet, the kids were sent to public schools, including high school. At that time, families were given the choice of which high school throughout the city their children could attend. A number of Terry's siblings attended nearby Lanier High, while the others, including Terry, took two city buses to Fox Tech.

As a young child, she was told by her father that she should become a nurse. At Tech, in addition to excelling at her academics, she took the nursing track very seriously, including becoming president of the Future Nurses Club. Friendly and outgoing, Terry volunteered for many school-related events, and even ran for high school class chaplain (but lost). During her senior year, as part of her home economics class, she was selected to be a model for a downtown women's clothing store.

It was also during this final year of high school that, as part of Mrs. Curran's speech class, Terry was chosen for the leading role in *Somewhere Over the Rainbow*. Decades later, she admitted to being oblivious to that boy staring at her all the time from backstage during rehearsals. She did recall, however, being quite flattered when he asked her out on a date, even if he had no shot at that time. "I was just trying to be polite," she said. "I had no intention of dating him nor anyone else."

"After a month or so, I decided to follow her around, and I discovered that she came to school early and went directly to the library," Juan said, adding that, on the day when he summoned enough courage to talk to her again, he found her on the library steps, as it was still closed, walked right up to her, and laid down this King of Romance pickup line: "You have the biggest tomato eyes I have ever seen." (Years later, Juan admitted to being quite nervous and shocked at himself that he'd said those words.)

Terry smiled. It certainly was an *original* thing to say, she thought. "I also thought that he was really serious about dating me," she said.

"After that day she'd speak to me, and eventually said that she would go on a date with me," said Juan. They went out many times, in fact, including whenever Terry needed someone to be with her during the family's civic club functions. They also went to prom together, with Juan working extra at Western Union to make enough money to rent a tuxedo.

"After many dates, we talked about plans for after graduation, and I found out that she was going to college to become a nurse," said Juan. "Of course, I told her that I, too, wanted to go to college."

Terry, however, had this recollection: "When we first met, he told me he was joining the military when he graduated."

One thing was for certain, Juan wasn't going to be a radio and TV repairman. After three years of trying, Juan proved incompatible with such a vocation. "I did not succeed in that class, and to this day I do not know the difference between a condenser and a receiver," he said. "I was a poor student. Since I did not know what my future would hold and I was not interested in anything in particular, the classes were not stimulating."

Nevertheless, Juan made the trip to the high school counselor, Jack Abbott, and told him that he wanted to go to college. "He was stunned," Juan remembered. But Abbott knew that Juan and Terry were dating, and being a very caring individual, he wanted to give Juan a chance to succeed. "He looked at my grades, which were mostly Ds, and advised me that San Antonio College, a junior college, would accept even students with my GPA."

As it turned out, San Antonio College, or "SAC," as everyone called it, was where Terry was all set to attend to get her nursing degree. So when SAC accepted Juan, he knew where his future would take him.

Juan, who had reclaimed his real name toward the end of senior year, was graduated from high school by a narrow academic margin, and then he joined his girlfriend at college. He needed to take refresher courses, including English 101, Math 101, and even something called Orientation 101. He got all Cs except for an A in math. The next semester he joined the data processing degree track and, for the first time in his life—what a difference a year and a good woman to support him made—he began excelling in his classes.

He also kept driving for Western Union, taking the opportunity to deliver to his sweetheart a Candygram on the appropriate occasions. It wasn't too long before he started making serious plans for the future, including marriage.

But there would be no wedding until after graduation. "Her father gave us that condition," Juan said, adding that it was simply to be expected in the Schultz household.

Terry's family followed traditional Hispanic values, especially when it came to the young women dating. In other words, when Juan first wanted to see Terry, he had to go through her dad first. Then, when they did go out, there were certain conditions that had to be met, as well, such as a curfew and several family chaperones, including her younger siblings, Mary G, Lisa, Tony, and nephews Don, Debbie, and Louie.

"I was 11 years old when I first met Juan Vasquez, around 1968," remembered Terry's brother Ray (Tony) Schultz. "My first memories of Juan are when he was courting my sister while they both were attending San Antonio College. My first reaction when Juan started coming over was: *brave man.*"

Terry's father sent them all along on Terry and Juan's dates, even though they couldn't do all that much as chaperones. Still, brother Ray was happy to fulfill his father's wishes for him to be a "third wheel" or "*chicle*" (meaning "gum," as in something that sticks around). His sister's dates took them to many drive-in theaters like the Mission, where they could get 10 hamburgers for $1. They also went to eat at the Malt House, the A&W for root beer floats, and long drives in the countryside. "The trips to the drive-in were the best times," said Ray. "Back then it only cost $2 a carload to get in, and Juan loaded up his car with many of my siblings. To us, Juan was the coolest person on the planet."

It wasn't all country drives and root beer floats, of course. Both Juan and Terry worked hard to pass their college courses. Juan had discovered determination within himself when it came to his classes and was even finding some of the work stimulating enough to think about possible jobs that might allow him to raise a family. Oh yes, even with a carload of *chicle*, Juan and Terry had begun to sketch out their futures, and, as it had finally been decided (even by Terry's father), their next steps were to be taken together.

In August 1969, Juan graduated with an associate's degree in data processing and stayed on at SAC to acquire transfer credits, intending to transfer to the University of Texas in Austin (UT) for a Bachelors of Business Administration degree with a major in accounting. On August 21, 1970, Terry graduated with a nursing degree (as she had promised her father she would before getting married). The following day, Saturday, August 22, they were married at Sacred Heart Catholic Church, on the West Side, with a small reception held at the American Legion Hall on Fredericksburg Road. Because Terry's grandfather Francisco Schultz had died on August 14, the wedding was almost cancelled. Even though the wedding ceremony went on, the reception was scaled down, although Terry persuaded her father to include a DJ.

For their honeymoon, the newlyweds drove to the Texas Gulf Coast and spent two nights in Galveston. "We decided to drive to New Orleans, and we ran out of money. Then we drove back using an Exxon credit card for gas and donuts," said Terry.

Back home, the new couple prepared to move to Austin, 80 miles away, so that Juan could attend UT.

They had said their goodbyes to their friends and families, plus Juan had delivered his last telegram. "I truly believe that working with Western Union helped form the determination that inspired me to work very hard and do my very best in the rest of my education," Juan said. And it would be a job that would always stay with him, as sure as picking cotton would remain forever in his consciousness. This job stretched his knowledge of the wider world while also providing perspective on his own hometown and his place within it.

With Terry, he had found something just as important as determination and twice as special. It was love, and it had already started changing Juan's life. It was like two people boarding a train. They await a journey without knowing their destination, yet they eagerly await the train to begin rolling.

CHAPTER SIX

The Long Road Home

Austin: August 1970 to May 1972

"I've been asked before if I was the first of my immediate family to go to college," said Juan. "Well, yes, I am, but I'm *actually* the first to make it through middle school."

It was with a sincere sense of dedication and responsibility—to his family, to the people who believed in him, to the people who couldn't even believe that Juan Vasquez *of all people* was attending the University of Texas at Austin—that he squared his shoulders, set his feet solidly beneath him, and faced his future.

With money saved from Juan's Western Union wages, the newlyweds bought a new mobile home and parked it at the University of Texas Trailer Park, lot number 65. The three-bedroom house lacked air conditioning (although they eventually installed a window unit), but it did have enough space for Juan to spread out and study.

"The UT Trailer Park was a wonderful place," Juan remembered. "Very nice. It was beautiful."

Lot number 65 would be the home base for the Vasquezes for two years. From there, Terry commuted to St. David's Hospital, where she worked as a nurse, and she loved it. Juan went to school and studied full time toward attaining an accounting degree, and he loved it. "I love learning, and I was good at numbers," Juan said. "In the cotton fields, I'd always be with my grandfather Flores. He wanted to make sure we got paid for every pound of cotton my family picked. I was there to do the math."

At UT, the problems were much more complicated, dealing with concepts and equations that a boy of nine, counting the family's cash for his grandfather, couldn't have begun to comprehend. There was so much effort that he needed to apply in order to understand what he was being taught, yet he never found a bottom to that energy. It was simply not to be exhausted. "I found that the harder I worked, the better my grades got. The return on my work came when I applied myself," he said.

What may seem to some students, and former students, as an obvious concept was to Juan, at that time, a fairly new discovery. As loving and caring as his families were, they weren't ever in a position to do anything other than make sure Juan actually *went* to school. After that, it was up to him to either apply himself or not. In the years leading up to his time at SAC, he mostly chose not to apply himself in the classroom. But, following that initial success with his data processing classes at junior college, things really started to change. It's important to note that he also had the support of someone who recognized the value of education because she felt it within herself and knew its benefits.

"Terry was on the honor roll in high school, always getting good grades," Juan pointed out. "It wasn't until I got to SAC, after the first semester of remedial classes, when I started making As. And as I remember, I started studying *more* than Terry. At some point, she'd be ready to close the books, maybe relax for the evening, but I'd insisted we stay and study more."

Terry remembered their time at UT as a period of seeing her husband go through this critical transition. It was a brightening period within him, with different parts of his brain lighting up and his imagination going to new, exciting places. "We were young. Juan wasn't really sure what he wanted to do for a career," Terry said. "But I could see him happy and motivated when this was happening."

Despite the long hours he put in at school and at home hitting the books, Juan was in love and he attended to Terry's happiness with similar devotion. There were date nights, and long talks about their future together. There were little gestures aimed to bring a smile to her face, like their first Valentine's Day as a married couple when he bought her a toy poodle (Lady Jennifer Michelle; "Jeannie" for short) to keep her company while he applied himself to his studies like never before. In return, Terry always assured Juan that she not only understood why he was working so hard, but also that she would do anything in her power to support him.

That motivation carried him through to his classes, where he continued to discover with delight why he'd always liked numbers: "You always come up to an answer. Numbers always come up with an answer. There might be some variances in how you get there, but there is one right answer. In accounting, the numbers have to jibe."

In his final year as an undergrad, finding himself approaching life after college, there was something both familiar and different about graduation this time around. He had entered UT as a wide-eyed young man and a newlywed, unsure of his future because he was unsure of himself. Now he was coming out of the university with not just skills, but also a desire for working with those skills. He knew he wanted to be an accountant, but as his final year continued, something wasn't quite right.

Terry remembered that time and said, "Because of the older Mexican American culture, we weren't ingrained to know to go to college in the first place, and so we didn't know what was going to be on the other side of that [graduation] door for Juan. It was a lack of education about what to expect, and we didn't know what was going to happen."

Specifically, Juan didn't know that companies, including accounting firms, came to the campus to recruit new employees. "I didn't realize what the Big 8 was," said Juan, referring to the eight largest accounting firms in the country at that time. Getting a job with one of the Big 8 companies was considered a crucial stepping-stone for anyone wanting to be a certified public accountant (CPA). Juan had already missed the interview with the accounting firm Arthur Andersen because he simply didn't know what it was or understand how the recruiting process worked. He finally caught on and interviewed with the next seven companies, which he felt was quite a competitive endeavor. Although he believed himself to be qualified because of his grades, which were As and Bs, during the interviews, he came to believe that his Mexican American heritage had led the interviewers to question his very ability to do the job. It was either that or they simply had a policy of not hiring men with brown skin to be accountants.

"The interviews would go something like this," Juan recalled: "What did your parents do, Juan?" Which seemed a fair question, one that most interviewers at the time could be expected to ask to get to know a little bit about the candidate. "Well, I lived with my grandparents, and we picked cotton for many years to support the family." And that would pretty much be the end of the interview. "Six of them rejected me."

The final firm was Lybrand, Ross Bros. & Montgomery (which later became Coopers and Lybrand, then PricewaterhouseCoopers, and is now PwC). That interview was going better than he had expected, but then Juan was asked if he would be willing to move to Los Angeles for work. He replied that he'd rather stay in Texas; after all, that firm had offices in Houston and Dallas. "They told me they didn't have openings there, which I found out later wasn't true. Other UT students got jobs there. But they were Caucasian."

To be sure, Juan was very proud of his achievements and his graduation from UT, but it had not escaped his notice that he was one of a very few number of Mexican American students in the business school. This was a time of great sociopolitical action by minorities across the country, including throughout Texas, as Hispanics were fighting to define themselves, to speak for themselves, and to be treated just like every other American citizen expected to be treated, especially in regards to the government and the law, but also within society itself. That included having the same opportunities as anyone else to get a good-paying job and build a better future than previous generations.

It was called the American Dream, and it was supposed to belong to all Americans, but minorities always had to fight for it.

Juan and Terry did not participate in any student walkouts or protest demonstrations. They didn't attend meetings or sign petitions. In time, their civic-mindedness would become a very important part of their lives together, but in early 1972, Terry was busy working and Juan had time for almost nothing other than his studies. It was his job to study and get that degree and, as Terry has said on dozens of occasions throughout their life together, it was her job to support him.

So when it became obvious that just about the only real opportunity to get a valuable entry position in his field was to move to Los Angeles—and this because of the color of his skin and his Mexican heritage—it was a bitter choice for him to make with Terry. "We didn't want to leave Texas," Juan said, "but I had no options."

Los Angeles: June 1972 to August 1974

The day had come when they had to sell their mobile home, say goodbye to the UT Trailer Park and lot number 65, and leave Texas. Their families were concerned for them—moving all the way across the country to California. And to smoggy Los Angeles of all places, home to over two million people; San Antonio didn't even have 700,000 people yet. The couple was nervous but had together found themselves excited too. They'd handled their first two years away from San Antonio with great success and had plenty left in the tank for Los Angeles.

Getting to LA included their first airplane ride, on Braniff Airlines. Upon their arrival, they moved in with uncle Adolph Flores and his wife, Laura, and lived with them for about three weeks until they found an apartment in Hollywood.

This was the home of Grauman's Chinese Theatre, the Walk of Fame, Musso & Frank Grill, Hollywood Boulevard, and the Sunset Strip. It was thriving with many different cultures, including a large and very visible Hispanic population. After renting for about three months, Juan and Terry bought a used double-wide mobile home, already located in the city of Paramount, south of Los Angeles. They were happy to have their own place, and Juan's college diploma was duly framed and hung on one of the walls of their new home. But the location, unfortunately, meant his commute to work in downtown LA took about an hour each way (despite the office being only 14 miles away).

In June, Juan, then a man of 140 pounds, who stood 5'7", joined the ranks of the pencil pushers at Lybrand, Ross Bros. & Montgomery, and he was not alone. There were about two dozen new hires, some of the brightest college accounting graduates in the country, who began working there as well. "They would call us 'pencil pushers,' which was true because we used to make notes on the statements with our pencils," said Juan.

But it was made known that perhaps half of that group could be gone before the next year began because new accountants were winnowed out—

fired—if they didn't show potential. Being a Mexican American as well as a first-year employee, Juan was on the bubble all the time.

Early on, he discovered that his audits were not very stimulating work. Minorities tended to be placed on audits of municipalities,[1] and Juan began his employment by auditing financials for hospitals and bus companies. There was little chance to get assigned the audit of, say, a big automaker, because those clients could choose their own auditors, and minorities were usually overlooked.[2] "I remember wanting to get on some better audits to have a possibility of making partner or growing with the company. What I got wasn't very challenging nor the type [of work] that gave me the opportunity for promotion," Juan said.

He also discovered that he wasn't always able to apply what he'd learned in school to the work. Although the numbers still came up with the one right answer, "In real accounting, people make mistakes," Juan explained. "In real life, when clients do things, they're human. You have to figure out the mistakes so as to make the numbers make sense. It wasn't as neat as in textbooks."

It wasn't exactly his dream job, but he still tried finding fulfillment in the work. "You have to make the best with what is given to you. You have to have faith—the faith in God and the faith of the family—to do the best you can. Always. So I still enjoyed working out the numbers," he said.

Then, during the tax season (January through April), he noticed a note on the employee bulletin board calling for volunteers to help out the tax department and prepare client tax returns. Juan volunteered and found the work to be more stimulating. "I remember looking at the clients' expenditures and having to determine how they're deductible. It's no longer black and white. I now had to ask *is* this expenditure deductible? Tax law works that way. I liked saving people money on their tax returns."

During this first year, Juan also made friends with fellow accountant Ed Winslow. Being an African American in this era, it was not unreasonable for Winslow to suspect that he could also be considered a candidate for a quicker exit when it came time for layoffs, because even within a company that hired minorities, it was much harder for those minorities, including Juan and Winslow, to rise through the ranks compared to Caucasians.[3] One day after work, when they were both coming out of the firm's building, they began talking. Winslow told Juan how he grew up with a single mom in "the projects" in nearby Compton. When Juan told of his cotton-picking background, Winslow doubled over laughing, saying, "And I thought I had it bad."

It broke the ice. The two became buddies at the office, and on occasion, like on a Friday or Saturday night, Winslow and his wife, Phyllis, would have dinner with Terry and Juan. They especially loved going out to a Mexican restaurant named El Cholo on Western Boulevard.

Winslow knew what was coming—the first-year layoffs—and he told Juan that they should both study together and take the LSAT (Law School Admission Test). It would give them more options; they would be worth more to the firm. Juan didn't know what the LSAT was, but he took his friend's advice and paid $40 to register for it. When Juan next ran into Winslow, a few weeks later at the office, Winslow told him that he, in fact, didn't register. Perhaps, Juan supposed, Winslow had changed his mind about his career path.

Left alone to study for admission to law school, something he'd simply never considered, Juan became very nervous about his prospects. He was also anxious about the way things were going at work. Many of his colleagues had been laid off.

At one point during his time volunteering in the tax department, Juan brought to the attention of a supervisor, Howard Schaefer, the issue of a client's specific deduction. Juan explained his position that while he didn't consider a particular item to be deductible for the reason that was indicated, he *did* believe the item could be deducted for a different reason. Impressed by Juan's work, Schaefer asked if he'd ever thought of law school.

Maybe that was a good sign—that others were recognizing and admiring the way he thought through problems; and, in fact, yes, by now he *had* thought of law school, and he intended to be thinking about it a lot more in the future. Just as importantly, he'd learned a lesson that he has since passed along from time to time: If you have to tell someone "no," try to also tell them how it can be done right.

In strategizing about his future, Juan asked Carl Moser, the partner in the tax department, if he could be transferred to his department. No, he was told, he could not transfer because he was not qualified. He needed a Master's of Business in Tax degree or a law degree before he would be considered for such a position.

He went home that same evening to discuss his thoughts with Terry. He thought it might be a tough conversation.

When the Vasquezes first moved to Los Angeles, Terry had been "scared to death" to begin work. "I didn't think I was prepared to work in the intense environment of the Los Angeles hospitals. So I took the summer off until I found a 16-week training course at St. Vincent's Medical Center." Following her training, she began working at St. Vincent's ICU and then the cardiac ICU unit. She took care of patients of all ages. "I loved it. It was very gratifying but very stressful. It came out naturally from me to help people get better. Being an RN has a lot of responsibility. Forget bathroom breaks. But it was very satisfying."

In addition to the fact that Terry had risen to the challenge of working in such a challenging environment, they had both taken full advantage of what Southern California offered, like the beaches and the food and maybe an occasional celebrity sighting. They traveled a lot, including driving a few hours to the mountains and flying for their first visit to the Hawaiian Islands. They had acclimated to living within the largest metropolitan area on the West Coast. "We loved LA," said Terry. Juan agreed: "We still love LA."

All that aside, the real bottom line, as they both had to admit at the time, was that Juan had simply not been given the appropriate opportunity to distinguish himself at such a large firm and his potential there was practically negligible. "I saw the writing on the wall," he said. "I, too, was going to be phased out by the end of the second year."

A master's program was a two-year commitment and a law degree required three more years in school. "That's a no-brainer," Terry declared to her husband. "There really isn't that much difference between two and three years. You'll go to law school."

Buffalo: August 1974 to May 1975

In mid-1974, the Vasquezes might have ended up moving to Boulder, Colorado, were it not for a simple scheduling conflict.

Based on Ed Winslow's encouragement, Juan had bought a book to study on his own for the LSAT. "Wrong way to do it," he admitted years later. "I didn't study right, but I wasn't going to let the $40 go to waste. It's better to take a review study course." As he sat for the exam, he realized it would take all his intelligence and willpower to do well, and with some clever thinking, he explained in the essay portion that the final test score (Juan was guessing that his score was going to be low) was not indicative of his existing skills, much less his potential.

Juan's score turned out to be pretty low, but he had applied to seven law schools, including some Ivy League universities. He was accepted to the Council on Legal Education Opportunity (CLEO) program at the University of Denver in Boulder, Colorado. It was a great moral boost to Juan's sense of accomplishment to have been accepted to law school. While anticipating another big change and a lot of grueling work, he dreamed with Terry about what life would be like living in the Rocky Mountain foothills.

But the CLEO program started in early June, and it was very important for Juan to fulfill his two-year CPA obligation as an accountant for his employer, now called Coopers & Lybrand. He simply couldn't leave work in time to attend school, and so he declined the offer.

But the State University of New York (SUNY) law school in Buffalo, New York, had also accepted him, and its classes started later in the fall. Juan accepted, which began the next leg of their journey.

"We were young and adventurous. We were ready to go somewhere else," said Terry about the cross-country move.

Their first foray to the East Coast—far away from their last home, not to mention San Antonio—was truly adventurous. The architecture was different. The food was different. The people were different. The weather, especially in winter, was very different. Having sold their home in Los Angeles to help with the costs of the move and school, they rented a small apartment near the Buffalo campus. At least the commute was a whole lot shorter.

In what may or may not have been a smart idea, shortly after being accepted to SUNY Buffalo, Juan and Terry watched the 1973 movie *The Paper Chase,* about the unbalanced life of a first-year law school student. It made Juan feel both scared and inspired. "It left an impression on me. Made me realize how difficult it was for those law school students—and *that's* what I was getting myself into," he said.

His first year of law school was, in fact, quite difficult. He had been out of an academic environment for two years. The reading volume alone was overwhelming. He had never felt so much like he was in a sink-or-swim environment like he did during those first two semesters in Buffalo. Plus, he was alone as a Mexican American in his classes. It was basically the same situation in his University of Texas accounting track, but this time it included much of the rest of the campus, not to mention the city of Buffalo. (Juan did join a Puerto Rican law student association for support from people who could at least empathize with such a cultural void.) The pressure and the work were so great that he lost 25 pounds that first year of his own paper chase. He also needed to get prescription glasses because of the enormous eye strain he'd developed from reading so many texts.

But Grandfather Flores had always lived by a certain work ethic, one that he instilled into his children and grandchildren as well: *If you're going to be a cotton-picker or a garbage collector or whatever, be the best.* Juan would hold tight to Apa's simple yet important advice all his life, even if his grandfather couldn't even conceive that his Juan would one day be taking that advice into college, much less law school. Still, Juan had heard Apa say, "*Sume la bota*" (Give it all you got) so many times in the cotton fields that he now heard it in his mind whenever there was a challenge to rise to. So from day one at school, Juan went into the business of studying again like it was his job; he buckled down and did his best to succeed. In due time, he learned how best to study, and the best way to study was to *always be studying*. "I studied, studied, studied. Terry tells me that I studied all of the time," said Juan. "And she was working a lot."

Upon their move from Los Angeles, Terry had originally found work in the coronary care unit of Buffalo's Millard Fillmore Hospital. But when she heard that the Veterans Administration (VA) hospital paid better, which was of vital importance to the couple, she transferred to the VA hospital's medical intensive care unit.

It was not just the financial support that Terry was providing that was of such help to Juan, but emotional support as well. Juan knew that, in fact, he was not alone in his journey, which made an incredible amount of difference in the outcome. "It turned out that I was okay because when the grades were posted after that first semester, I sighed with relief that I had passed and made an honors grade in Criminal Law."

Juan and Terry drove home to San Antonio for a couple of weeks before the start of the next semester. It would prove to be a very important trip, in part because it allowed them to enjoy time with their families, soak in some of the Texas sunshine, and visit some familiar old haunts. They also found time to see friends, including Eduardo "Eddie" Saenz, who was attending his first year at the University of Houston Law Center. Saenz asked Juan where he was planning to practice law after graduation.

The question made Juan think. While he'd believed that it was likely they would move back to Texas for his work, it made Juan realize that SUNY Buffalo didn't teach community law nor oil and gas law, which would be on the Texas bar exams and would be highly beneficial for any lawyer in Texas. Saenz also discussed how the University of Houston law school had a lot of diversity, including about 10 Mexican American first-year students enrolled, and that he was involved in increasing enrollment with the Chicano Law Student Association there. Saenz thought Juan would be an excellent addition.

Terry and Juan returned to Buffalo for the second semester, which continued to be a struggle but which also continued to bring academic success. "My impression *now*," said Juan, more than forty years after making it through his first year of law school, "is when you take first-year students, no matter how smart they are, their minds are mush. The professor has to mold that mind to *think* like a lawyer. That first year is so important."

Juan did a lot of thinking about his second year, and after discussing his options with Terry, they decided Juan should apply to the Bates Law Center at the University of Houston, now called the University of Houston Law Center. They also decided that it was as good a time as any to start a family. On the day that they were moving across the street to a bigger, two-bedroom apartment in preparation for a baby, a letter arrived from the University of Houston: Juan had been accepted. Classes started in two months. Plans for a baby were put on hold.

Houston: September 1975 to May 1977

In September 1975, there were only ten or eleven students, including Juan, in Professor Ira Shepard's evening Corporate Tax class, and each person tended to choose the same seat each lecture. Paul Dostart and Juan sat next to each other for many long hours of Shepard's lectures. Over time, they got to know one another a bit. They quickly surmised that they had different upbringings from different backgrounds in different parts of the country. (Dostart grew up on a farm in Iowa and was a National Merit Scholar in high school.)

But even more curious was that while Juan had never thought much about having a legal career until just a few years prior, Dostart had been set on being a lawyer since he was a kid. "There was never a doubt in mind what I wanted to do once I became aware that I could actually choose my own career," Dostart said.

Although the two young men's levels of confidence—feeling like this was exactly where to be at this exact time in life—were at opposite ends of the spectrum, their determination to succeed—because this is exactly what was needed to be done at this exact time in life—was certainly on equal ground.

They also had something else in common: they were both CPAs. In fact, Dostart was also teaching accounting in the school of business while attending law school. So they could discuss the black-and-white nature of accounting verses the myriad ways of interpreting tax laws.

Notably, at the University of Houston in 1975, Juan stated, there were only ten Hispanics in the entire law school. He also remembered that this group bonded over their cultural heritage ("They all came from the outlying areas of Texas, including South Texas," Juan said), but they also bonded over the law. "We were learning about the law and how we can fight for the rights of all Americans, including Mexican Americans."

Such considerations were important because the Mexican American civil rights struggles had accomplished much across the country and in Texas. But many understood that just because basic rights for minorities and a guarantee of equality under the law had been legislated by Congress and upheld by the Supreme Court, it didn't mean that in practice Hispanics, for instance, were being treated much differently.[4] While Juan and Terry had basically kept their focus on simply surviving as a family—their first son, Juan Jr. (Juanito) was born on August 28, 1976—while they endured the third year of law school, they certainly believed in racial equality and would continue to acknowledge their responsibilities to ensure that all Americans were treated with dignity and equality.

Most of Juan's corporate tax classmates worked during the day. So Shepard's class was taught at night. In it, Juan found that he was developing something like a passion for tax law, and he wasn't alone. Dostart has similarly fond memories of that class: "Ira Shepard inspired both Juan and me and, I dare say, several others. He was an enthusiastic tax professor. He was a fun guy. He made tax fun."

It was during class, while sitting next to Juan so often, that Dostart noticed that Juan took copious notes, which was normal. "But I noticed that it wasn't English. And I knew very little Spanish at the time, but I didn't think it was Spanish either," said Dostart. "Later, I asked Juan about it, thinking it was some kind of shorthand."

Juan explained that, even though he grew up speaking Spanish, he didn't read or write Spanish very well. His whole academic career had obviously been in English, yet the translator voice in his head often defaulted to Spanish. "So what he was taking notes in was neither fully English nor Spanish," said Dostart. "And at night, Juan told me, Terry would work with him to translate what he had written and help write everything out again in English. It's really a testament to Juan's perseverance and work ethic that he went through all that when the rest of us didn't have that issue to contend with."

Shepard, whom Juan in time would consider a mentor and friend, as well as his teacher, was impressed with Juan's work ethic and grades and made him his teaching assistant for the summers of 1976 and 1977. "I worked with him for the Southern Federal Tax Institute (SFTI)," said Juan. The SFTI is a nonprofit organization for accountants, attorneys, and financial professionals that provides in-depth information on current topics of interest in the field of tax law, and Shepard was a special advisor to the institute. "My job was to proofread the many articles submitted to the Southern Federal Tax Institute for Ira's review."

Considering what Juan had to contend with concerning his particular challenge of language, it showed remarkable faith to have Juan tackle that job. It also showed how proficient and capable Juan had become in his specific area of the law.

"One day, I recall, Ira Shepard spoke with me at length about how I needed to pursue my tax education and get my master's in tax, called an LL.M. in tax, from New York University [NYU]," Juan said. "Of course, I was very pleased of this compliment, but I needed to speak with Terry. And of course, we had our son, Juan Jr., who was about nine months old."

In fact, although Juan and Terry understood that getting an extra degree would be beneficial in the long run of Juan's career, before applying to NYU, Juan looked for an attorney job in San Antonio. During one such interview, Juan was again asked what his parents did for a living. Again, he explained how his mother died of tuberculosis, how he was raised by his two families, and that the Flores family picked cotton. "But this time," said Juan, "the interviewer told me, 'My family owns a lot of cotton fields in South Texas, and so maybe your family picked cotton for my family.'" He was not offered the position.

Juan took the Texas bar exam in February 1977 and received his passing results in June. The Vasquez family celebrated Juan's success with a weekend in Galveston with friend and fellow University of Houston student Marcelo Montemayor and his wife, Janet.

New York City: September 1977 to May 1978

Juan and Paul Dostart both graduated with their Juris Doctor (J.D.) degrees in 1977 from the University of Houston Law Center, and both moved to New York City to attend NYU for their LL.M.s. (The abbreviation stands for "Legum Magister" and means Master of Laws.)

"NYU was a very happy time in our lives," said Joyce Dostart. In Houston she had married Paul Dostart in 1976, was a nurse anesthetist, and became good friends with Juan and Terry. When they all moved to New York, they even lived in the same apartment building (Hayden Hall), a married-student housing high-rise in Greenwich Village. "It was a time of hope and promise. It was exciting to be there. It was all of our first time in New York City."

Juan and Terry's apartment was a very small, narrow, one-bedroom unit with a kitchenette. Since Juanito was only 11 months old when they moved in, the family slept in the same room. Within a couple of months, when it became obvious that three was a crowd, the adults' mattress was moved out of the bedroom and into the living room. Such logistics hardly mattered to them, though. It's safe to say that, by that time, Terry and Juan knew how to play the graduate school game. Even with Juanito to care for, even while living in the heart of New York City, even while attending the prestigious New York University for an advanced degree, none of it was enough to deter them now.

"We did not go anywhere during the first semester because I was always studying. The material was super hard," said Juan. "But we did pick up a slice of pizza on Friday or Saturday nights and ate in our apartment, on our sofa, after our son was asleep. We loved to look out the large window of our living room and enjoy the beauty of the lights from the twin towers of the World Trade Center. As for the second semester, we joined a babysitting group in the building. This is where Paul and Joyce Dostart helped a lot."

"We got to know the city, particularly Manhattan, pretty well. We were young and full of energy," said Joyce Dostart. "Sometimes we would babysit Juanito, while Terry and Juan went out. I loved that time of life and look back fondly upon it. All four of us were amazed at what we could find in the city."

Taking whatever time off they could get, Juan and Terry explored New York City, yet another, even bigger, city to call home. They even took the subway to see Broadway plays, including *The King and I* (with Yul Brenner), and *Hello, Dolly!* (starring Carol Channing.)

It wasn't all plays and pizza, of course. While Juan studied and attended class, Terry worked part-time in the coronary care unit at St. Vincent's Hospital Manhattan. She worked nights, and because the hospital was located only two blocks from the apartment, she walked to and from work, though she didn't necessarily always feel safe.

Juan came closer to receiving his degree, although he was amazed at the level of intelligence of his fellow students. In October 2017, for the video feature "Texas Tax Legends," by the State Bar of Texas, Tax Section, Juan told William Elliott, "I had prepared tax returns, [I was a] CPA, I had taken corporate tax [class] with Ira [Shepard]. … I thought I was a tax hotshot. And when I got to NYU, it's a good thing I didn't advertise it. I realized there were so many smart people at NYU. Incredibly smart. The NYU tax program is not for wimps. You have to work hard."

Getting through the year would be another major accomplishment on many levels, not the least of which was overcoming doubt. It was common that being raised a Mexican American in the Caucasian majority often led to a lack of self-confidence, especially in the areas of higher education. While both Juan and Terry had in the backs of their minds the idea that they would return to Texas upon graduation, they also knew now that they were capable of living just about anywhere. And wouldn't the best thing be to follow the best opportunity for Juan? (For Paul Dostart, the best opportunity awaited in Southern California; so he and Joyce moved to San Diego after graduation.)

Juan was offered a full-time position with the Department of Justice (DOJ) Tax Division in Washington, D.C. It was, of course, a good job opportunity, and it would mean yet another new destination for the Vasquez family to tackle. Although they didn't know it at the time, Juan *would* eventually have an office for his work in Washington, D.C. But that was still years away. In 1978 Juan felt the pull of Texas, and so he declined the offer.

Houston: August 1978 to August 1982

About the same time, Juan was also offered a position in Texas with the Internal Revenue Service Office of Chief Counsel. Juan accepted the offer even though it hadn't been determined to which city he would be assigned. Later, when Juan traveled to Washington D.C. to receive his official assignment, he learned he would be returning to Houston and his first day of work would be August 7.

Before they moved their family back to Texas, Juan and Terry embarked on several trips around the country, their first vacation in a long time. They first flew to visit Juan's sister, Sylvia, and her family in Tacoma, Washington, and then flew to Los Angeles, where they bought a car from Juan's uncle, Adolph Flores: (actually, it was an orange 1974 Dodge van with orange shag carpet and two black captain chairs. They then drove to Long Beach and visited Terry's sister Sylvia Zoet and her family before driving across the country to visit some sites in Florida. After returning to San Antonio for a week, they finally drove to and parked their orange family van in Houston.

Juan returned to the working world, and in his job with the Chief Counsel he learned exactly how the tax laws written by Congress were litigated between private citizens and their government. Juan generally worked on U.S. Tax Court cases involving deficiencies in estate taxes, gift taxes, and income taxes.

Judges for the U.S. Tax Court, created by Congress to adjudicate these disputes, travel to Houston about eight to ten times a year,[5] and it was the responsibility of attorneys such as Juan to prepare the cases to go to court and assist the IRS when needed. The cases and files that he worked on consisted of everyday situations arising when petitioners were not satisfied with the result of previous findings from other IRS divisions, including the Audit and Appeals Departments. Other cases included assignments for Tax Court litigation and collection.

"The trial sessions are a lot of work for the office," Juan explained. "They have to prepare all the cases for the time. The IRS attorneys have many cases to try during these sessions because the Tax Court can only be in the area, in this case Houston, for so long before it moves to its next city. You can't try them all; so you have to settle some of them." (In private practice, the attorney for the taxpayer might only have one case per session.)[6]

At last, after so many years spent grinding out an education, Juan was a working professional in his chosen field. And as a public servant, he enjoyed and excelled at his work.

"When I worked for the Chief Counsel, I really had to do my best on those cases. You have to know that case better than anyone in the office. You *should* know it as well as the petitioners.

"Today, I tell students that [IRS] attorneys would occasionally get a 'dog' of a case, not that interesting, not that complicated. But if you do your best with that case, it shows others how hard you're willing to work and they'll be more willing to give you better cases. But don't fool yourself. You know when you did your best and when you didn't. I learned so much from my grandfather."

Of the hundreds and hundreds of lawyers working for the Chief Counsel's office throughout the country, only a handful were Hispanic.[7] In addition to

Juan's duties as a lawyer, he'd been asked to bring that number up by being a part of what he referred to as a "quiet program" of visiting a number of universities in Texas and other western states to recruit Hispanics and other minorities. This became a very important aspect to Juan's work, and he took this extremely seriously, conveying to young law students how critical it was not only to be knowledgeable of the role the government plays in tax law but also to be a part of the system itself. Juan was able to recruit a sizable number of minorities before he resigned his position and was acknowledged to have a pivotal role in bringing diversity to the Chief Counsel's office.

In addition to being proud of her husband, Terry had found great satisfaction in raising Juan Jr. while also working at the VA in Houston. "I had a great, perfect job in the medical intensive care unit; then I got transferred to the surgical intensive care unit and then to the cardiac catheterization laboratory," she said. "This was such fulfilling work, just Monday through Friday, and no calls on the weekends. That's ideal for a nurse."

In his years representing the government, Juan won all but one of his cases and had been recognized for his extra-administrative activities. After his four-year commitment was up, though, he found that he still had a yearning to go back to San Antonio.

This pull had certainly been increased after grandfather Jesus Flores passed away on October 30, 1981, at the age of 86. Without a doubt, Apa Flores had been a significant influence in Juan's life, representing many of the qualities that he tried to live by, would instill in his own children, and would eventually pass on to those whom he would mentor professionally.

So when the time came to again make decisions about the future, Juan decided that he wanted to practice law and be close to his family in his hometown.

Terry actually raised a protest. "Because I had finally achieved the ultimate position as a nurse. I was so happy," she explained.

But Juan said, "I want to go home."

CHAPTER SEVEN

Private Practice, an Introduction to the Arts, and When the "Big One" Hit

"I understood and shared Juan's longing to go home," said Terry, remembering their conversation toward the end of their time living in Houston. "I did have a great job, one that I had worked hard to get, but we both wanted to move back to our beloved San Antonio."

While still planning the logistics of the move, Juan interviewed with several tax firms in San Antonio, but despite his years as a practicing attorney with the government, he was again confronted with rejections. In one interview, he was told that he was "too qualified" with all the advanced degrees and experience he had earned. Ironically, that firm was the same one that had rejected him twice after he'd graduated from law school and had received his LL.M. in Tax at NYU.

During the final months of his tenure with the IRS Chief Counsel in Houston, he met Leonard Leighton, a San Antonio attorney who was representing a client in a case on which Juan was working on the other side. "Leonard had a private practice in San Antonio. I was impressed with him and how he worked. Once that case was over, I got in contact with him. I probably called and asked if I could meet with him in San Antonio. After that meeting he made me an offer," said Juan.

When the Vasquez family returned to San Antonio, they returned as a family of four. Jaime had been born in Houston on April 21, 1981, and was a little over the age of one, while Juan Jr. was about to turn six when the family moved into their new house, north of downtown, about five miles from Juan's new office. It was also close to St. Luke's Hospital, where Terry found work in the cardiac catheterization laboratory and the radiology department.

It was 1982. It had been 12 years since they last lived in San Antonio, and naturally some things still felt like home. But even though they weren't living in a more familiar part of town, Juan and Terry could still easily see and recognize that things had changed and were continuing to evolve within their hometown.

"It was exciting because Hispanics were starting to become more visible and have more responsibilities in government and throughout the city," said Juan, citing that Henry Cisneros was mayor and the first Mexican American to serve in that role in San Antonio since 1842. (Cisneros would later serve as Secretary of Housing and Urban Development under President Bill Clinton.)

Terry agreed, "It was a good time to move back because of the opportunities. Some of our friends who were Hispanic were also attorneys in private practice."

When Juan joined Leighton and his partner, Larry Hood, in August 1982, two things immediately happened. "When I joined [Leonard] it became Leighton, Hood and Vasquez. "I wasn't a partner yet, but he did it for marketing purposes." Juan said. "I also took a 25 percent pay cut to join. I often joke that I'm the only person I know who took a pay cut from the government to go into private practice. But Leonard was very business-minded, and he gave me 25 percent commission for the new work I brought in. I knew I would have to really hustle to make it work."

Essentially, Juan was doing the same kind of work as when the government was his employer, only now he was on the other side. He prepared his cases *against* the IRS rather than for them. It's a fairly advantageous position to be in because he was well aware of what the government attorneys would be doing the days before their date in Tax Court, specifically, working on many other cases at the same time. He was familiar with the legal arguments that would come his way, and most importantly he knew the law. As for learning the rest of what it meant to be successful in private practice, Leighton was there to instruct.

"He was a great guy," said Terry of Leighton, who died in 2013. "He taught Juan a lot. But Juan still had to get his name out there. So wherever we went, out came the cards."

Juan handed out his business cards to just about anyone he thought could be a potential client, and he joined a number of organizations such as the Hispanic Chamber of Commerce, the Hispanic Business Association, the San Antonio Bar Association, the State Bar of Texas, the Mexican American Bar Association of San Antonio, the Mexican American Bar Association of Texas, the Hispanic National Bar Association, and the American Bar Association, Tax Section, in order to network with the kind of people who might have the particular legal needs that Juan could provide.

He was never without his cards and certainly had them on him during a chilly November morning when he was on his way to the office but decided to stop in at a small restaurant, La Fogata, to grab some coffee and a taco. "I remember that day because it was pretty cold for San Antonio," Juan said. "La Fogata had five tables inside, and when I got there all the tables were taken."

He spotted a table with only one person sitting at it and moved toward it. Who knows? he thought, the man seated there might need some legal work done.

"You have to understand," Juan explained, "this is the first time I was ever in private practice. So I was always looking for clients. I'd meet people and give them a card and say, 'If you have problems with the IRS, give me a call.' "

He was all ready to deliver his usual introduction and asked the man at the table if it would be okay to sit down. The man looked up from his coffee with a bit of a perturbed look and replied, "Well, if you *have* to."

It wasn't the most welcoming welcome, but Juan thanked him and took a seat to eat some breakfast. He then noticed that the man had a prosthetic, a silver clamp, where his right forearm and hand should be. After a few moments, Juan introduced himself. The man said his name was Jesse Treviño, but otherwise he mostly stayed silent, as if deep in thought.

"It was hard to get a conversation going," Juan remembered. "I had to draw things out of him. Finally, I asked him what he did for a living."

Treviño looked up, almost like he couldn't believe what he was hearing. Finally, he said that he was an artist, "a real artist." In fact, he told Juan that he was something of a *famous* artist,[1] who had studied in New York.

Having earned his LL.M. from NYU, Juan also knew something about New York. In a moment of levity, he said, "Well, I am a *famous* attorney because I studied at the New York University School of Law." His joke worked, and Treviño began to open up a bit as they talked about New York.

It turned out that Treviño was, in fact, a famous artist. Or at least getting famous pretty quickly. Born in Mexico and raised in San Antonio's West Side neighborhood of Prospect Hill (a couple blocks from where Terry grew up), Treviño had been studying on a scholarship at the Art Students League of New York when he was drafted into the army in 1966 for the Vietnam War. Badly injured in the Mekong Delta, the result of a landmine and sniper fire, he underwent several surgeries for life-threatening wounds to his right leg and right arm. Eventually, his right arm below the elbow was amputated and replaced with a prosthetic. Yet, Treviño didn't quit on his artistic dreams. Training himself to paint left-handed, he rebuilt his career, eventually earning widespread acclaim as a photorealist painter of the people and places of San Antonio's West Side. He was considered one of the city's most exciting artists and an important figure in America's Chicano Art Movement.[2]

"Jesse told me that he had just finished painting *Imagines de Mi Pueblo* (*Images of My Town*) at what used to be the West Side Bank," Juan said, referring to Treviño's 54-foot-long mural in the lobby of what is now Wells Fargo Bank on Castroville Road. "I told him that Terry had worked at that bank, in the back office, reviewing checks."

Before long, the two discovered they had even more in common, like that they both attended Fox Tech. Treviño was two years older than Juan and

Terry, and they didn't remember one another from high school, but their conversation turned out to be as satisfying as the food they were enjoying. Eventually, Juan had to leave to get to work but not without first giving the artist his business card, of course.

The next morning Juan found himself looking forward to another breakfast at La Fogata. When he arrived, there was Treviño, sitting by himself again. Juan joined him, and they talked some more. The same thing happened the next day and the day after. In fact, they began regularly meeting for breakfast together at La Fogata for many years.

In time, Juan introduced Terry to Treviño, who was dating a woman named Theresa, also called Terry. The four of them occasionally went on double dates. Sometimes Treviño introduced them to his world, one of art and artists. It was much different than their professional circle of attorneys, but Juan and Terry enjoyed learning about this creative community. "We didn't grow up with that kind of culture," Terry said. "We didn't grow up with art."

In turn, Juan introduced Treviño to attorneys and business professionals, whom he'd gotten to know through his law practice; some of them would commission paintings from Treviño.

After that first encounter at La Fogata, and through their continued breakfast meetings, both Juan and Treviño realized that they had a lot in common beyond being alumni of the same high school and previously living in New York. Most of all, says Juan, "There was mutual understanding of where they came from and that the both of us had high aspirations."

It didn't take that long before Juan and Terry found themselves truly enthusiastic about art, especially Treviño's work. One of his paintings in particular, *Guadalupe y Calaveras* (1976, acrylic on canvas, 66" × 48") was a piece that Juan found himself growing quite fond of. The painting shows a gas station, once located at the intersection of Guadalupe and Calaveras in San Antonio, where Terry grew up, with several men huddled around a couple of cars at the filling pumps. It was a typical scene found on the West Side, but really, it felt like a setting that could take place anywhere: a portrait of people coming together to talk of how their day was going so far, swapping stories from work, and getting the *really* local neighborhood information, the kind not found in newspapers. Like this painting, much of Treviño's work is celebrated for showing the people and places of the West Side, yet portrayed with a broader appeal.

Terry, who was just as enthusiastic about Treviño's art as Juan, was slightly shocked when her husband—seemingly out of the blue—announced that he wanted to buy *Guadalupe y Calaveras*. "I said yes," said Terry, which slightly shocked her husband in return. "My dad owned and worked at a gas station for a while before he went into the navy, and it looked like the one in the painting," she said.

Then Juan told Terry the price: Treviño wanted $9,000.[3] Despite the fact that they were doing well at work, while raising their family they just couldn't afford $9,000. Still, they both truly wanted it, and both felt that they simply *had* to have it. That's how strongly they felt about their burgeoning art appreciation. In the end, Treviño appreciated their passion, and because they were all friends, he kept his price the same but allowed them to pay in installments.

As they hung their new purchase at Juan's law office, Juan and Terry felt proud and excited to officially become art collectors. Having made their first high-value art acquisition, they were far from being through. Although art from other artists appealed to them, over the years, as their friendship with Treviño grew, they would collect several of his works, including a set of sketches from his time at the Art Students League.

Their family would also commission original paintings from the artist; perhaps the most special piece is one they commissioned in 1984. Juan wished to commemorate grandfather Jesus Flores, who instilled an enduring hard-working spirit in Juan. He supplied Treviño with photographs of Jesus Flores as well as some images of what one would see, such as the equipment used, while working the fields. One day, having heard Juan's stories of his time in the cotton fields, Treviño asked for any photos Juan had from that time of his life, which might help with his research.

When the painting was completed and unveiled, there stood grandfather and grandson, side by side, working in an endless field of cotton. Both Jesus and Juan carried full sacks of cotton over their shoulders. A scale mounted on a tripod was set off to the side, as was Don Trini's truck, always waiting for the pickers to finish a row and empty their sacks, and then take the cotton to the gin. It was called *Los Piscadores* (*The Pickers*; 1985, acrylic on canvas, 82" × 48"), and when Juan saw it for the first time—and saw himself immortalized on canvas with his grandfather—he nearly wept.

It was such a powerful painting that it was loaned to Richard Anthony "Cheech" Marin, comedian, actor, and art collector, for his Chicano Visions: American Painters on the Verge national exhibition tour (2001–2007), showcasing some of Marin's favorite Chicano artists.[4] Juan and Terry wanted to keep an eye on their painting and traveled to 12 of the show's locations as it toured the country, including Washington, D.C., San Diego, San Francisco, and Fort Lauderdale.[5] Since many of the show's pieces belonged to Marin, he often gave personal tours of the exhibition when it stopped in a new location, and he soon learned to expect to run into Juan and Terry. Juan and Terry both remember Marin speaking fondly of *Los Piscadores* and explaining the story behind the painting. Then he'd point to Juan and introduce him as the young boy in the painting, explaining why the piece truly represented the American Dream.[6]

Meanwhile, Juan kept working hard for Leighton and was officially made a partner in the law firm. After five profitable years, however, they both came to the same conclusion that it was time for Juan to strike out on his own. Juan ended up renting space from Leighton in the same building, just upstairs. That's where he first truly hung his shingle: Juan F. Vasquez, a Professional Corporation.

Although neither Juan nor Terry recall the exact moment Juan began signing his name "Juan *F.* Vasquez," he knew it was often customary in Hispanic culture to use the mother's maiden name as a middle name. By the time he went into practice for himself, it was Juan Flores Vasquez who had gained such a solid reputation from his clients and colleagues.

Juan hired a staff, including his administrative assistant, Lisa Rodgers-Schneider, and attorneys Cristina Carter and Gary Alonzo. He also worked diligently to build a strong client list, and it wasn't unusual for a client to stay a client for years and refer others to Juan. Some clients became friends. His business became successful enough that after six years, Juan chose to work solo.

Juan's easygoing manner endeared him to clients and other attorneys as much as his knowledge of the law, recalled Robert E. McKenzie, of Saul Ewing Arnstein & Lehr in Chicago. "I first met Juan in 1986. I was teaching a tax representation seminar in San Antonio," said McKenzie. "After the seminar he approached me and asked when I was scheduled to return to Chicago. When he learned that I had a late flight home, he asked me to dinner. We went to the Old Town and had great fajitas. During that dinner our friendship blossomed. We had a lot in common. We had both begun our careers with the IRS and later entered private practice. Both of us formed our own small tax firms. We also learned that we had been raised in very poor working-class families and had been the first to attend law school. That bond of friendship, formed over fajitas, between two men who came up the hard way, endures to this day."

One day, a man came to his office for a consultation and asked how much it would cost. When Juan told him the price for his services, the man decided to look for another tax attorney. The next week, that same man came back and hired Juan. When Juan inquired why he'd returned, the new client responded that after asking around he found out that Juan had a reputation of being the "best tax attorney for the little people."

It's very possible that that particular client had been to see, among other attorneys, Chad Muller. Muller had a stellar reputation for his work and was in demand for his services. "I was with a firm called Matthews and Branscomb, and I was at a point in my career where I was charging a significant amount for representation," said Muller. "I know of a story where another attorney once had asked Juan how he competed with me in San Antonio, when I would get all the big cases, charging a $50,000 retainer. Juan responded that he only charged $5,000 retainers—but there are a whole lot more of those than $50,000 retainers. I really don't think for Juan it was about the money necessarily; it's a desire to help people who were caught up in the tax system and just didn't know how to get out. They were struggling, and he wanted to help them."

With his growing reputation—and client list—Juan was becoming quite busy with work. His son Jaime said of the time, "I remember my dad working all the time in private practice. He would bring work home. He would work at night. He would bring work on vacations."

Juan Jr. even caught on to Juan's agenda behind some of those vacations: "I remember realizing during one of our family trips that Dad would have to leave for a few hours, and it occurred to me that he was attending work conferences. It wasn't uncommon at all for our vacations to also be business trips for him."

Juan admitted this to be the case, explaining that his job simply required him to constantly be working, to be learning, and to be looking for new clients *and* new contacts. "I kept going to conferences as usual, and I met with other lawyers and gave them my card and told them to give me a call if they had IRS problems for their clients," Juan explained. "I would go to accountants and tell them that I don't do tax returns, so I'm not competing with them, but if they had problems with the IRS to call me."

Always on display throughout his career was Juan's natural curiosity of other people, and their journeys through life. In later years, this attentiveness and empathy would serve him well. "My wife, Gail, and I met Juan and Terry in the 1980s at an ABA Tax Section meeting in Washington, DC," says tax attorney Martin Press, shareholder at Gunster in Fort Lauderdale. "They were new to the Tax Section. We soon discovered that, even though we came from different states and different backgrounds, we had a lot in common. We were both married a week apart in 1970. Gail and I came from Jewish New York roots, and Terry and Juan came from Mexican Texas, Roman Catholic backgrounds. We shared the same values of educational achievement that would lead to the American Dream of a professional career helping people and our country along the way."

In January 1994, Juan and Terry traveled to Los Angeles to attend the annual University of Southern California Tax Institute, a three-day tax conference, for Juan's continuing legal education in tax certification. Juan attended the various seminars, handed out countless business cards, and spoke with many people in his field. It was a fairly typical event. After the day's classes were over, Juan and Terry returned to Casa Malibu, a small Malibu hotel close to the Pacific Ocean. Each evening they walked the beach and watched the waves crash onto the shore as the sun set over the horizon. It was during these walks that the conversation often drifted away from the work of the day and more toward their future.

"Deep within my soul, I felt that there must be something else that Juan and I could contribute to the world and our communities," said Terry of that time. "It is kind of hard to explain, but that is the best way that I can describe it in words. Juan and I spoke about these feelings often."

"Terry brought to my attention that she was concerned that I had reached my maximum in my profession and my solo practice," Juan said. "She questioned if there was anything else out there for me." He had been talking to other tax professionals about joining a bigger tax firm in San Antonio. He'd also been counseled by Lewis Hubbard, from the IRS Chief Counsel office in

Austin, that he should consider a Tax Court judgeship because of a current vacancy.

"Wow, I was shocked that he even brought it up because, honestly, we both felt a judgeship was simply beyond our reach, beyond our expectations," Terry said. "Besides, we knew nothing about the position. Basically, we benched the idea for the rest of this California trip, but decided to discuss it further with other professionals when we went back home."

The following morning, at about 4:30, the 6.7 magnitude Northridge Earthquake upended parts of Southern California, including Malibu.[7] In their hotel room, Juan and Terry were abruptly awakened with the bed and room violently shaking. It seemed like the jolts and rolling would never end. They could hear the windows rattling and glass breaking in the nearby kitchenette. Although seismic activity lasted only about 15 seconds, the rumbling felt like it continued for many long minutes. They had experienced a few minor earthquakes when they previously lived in Los Angeles, but those were absolutely nothing like what shook their Malibu room. Finally, the movement stopped, leaving their room eerily quiet and dark. Soon, voices outside their room confirmed the activity had been an earthquake, and apparently everybody nearby was safe.

Dawn was punctuated by several large aftershocks, but as daylight arrived, Juan and Terry quickly packed, found their car, and slowly made their way through traffic to the airport: they had a plane back to San Antonio to catch and they weren't about to miss it.

Just as soon as they we safely in the air and on their way back home, they decided it was probably best to not take the earthquake as any kind of a prognostication about their future. On the other hand, they weren't going to rule anything out.

CHAPTER EIGHT

The Judgeship Journey

The portrait of Juan F. Vasquez in the *American Dream* at Mi Tierra shows him looking quite distinguished in his judge's robe. The expression on his face suggests he is a man who is both proud of where he came from and determined to be successful in the future. His shoulders are straight, even with the weight from all those who came before him, those who sacrificed for him, those who loved him no matter what became of him, resting heavy upon them.

American Dream also shows him as a nine-year-old child, with an expression of pride from being a strong worker helping his family. Apa, Jesus Flores, stands with him, and when Apa tells him, *"Sume la bota,"* Juan responds with all he's got. His shoulders are hunched forward, carrying his own weight and ready to take on more.

This portrait was painted by San Antonio artist Robert Ytuarte in 2014. Over the shoulder of Juan's adult likeness as a judge, Ytuarte has included *Los Piscadores*, Jesse Treviño's painting of Juan and Jesus Flores in the cotton fields of South Texas. It is an elegant and appropriate juxtaposition, since Juan's early experiences influenced what he would become later in life, and because his grandfather's words of determination, "Always do your best," never left him as he pushed against societal limitations and his own personal insecurities to continue moving steadily down the path to success and fulfillment.

Even when they were back home telling their family, friends, and colleagues about their trip to California—especially how the "Big One" struck in the early morning as they slept in Malibu—Juan and Terry just couldn't bring themselves to assign any supernatural intention to the earthquake. But something more important did happen: They both returned to San Antonio with the notion of Juan taking another bold step in his career, this time by exploring the possibility of obtaining a judgeship on the United States Tax Court.

Attorney and friend Chad Muller had no doubt that Juan was competent and qualified for such a position. "Juan was always well informed about changes in the law and was very professional about staying in touch with those changes," he said. "Probably the most important thing was his commitment to helping people who are struggling with the law."

Others had also expressed their confidence that Juan should make the attempt, which bolstered his belief that he, Terry, and his family would be able to work through any of the challenges that such an endeavor would bring. They truly had no idea what those challenges would actually be, but years later, when looking back on the whole chaotic ordeal that did unfold, Juan and Terry often described this time as feeling something like being on a runaway train.

In a sense, they boarded that train when Juan committed himself to the challenge. He knew his desired destination, a judgeship, but didn't know how to get there. Juan hoped the ABA Tax Section Midyear Meeting, in Houston in January 1994, would be the right place to seek a little clarity. Juan had been very active with the ABA Tax Section ever since fellow tax attorney Chad Muller had introduced him to the organization in 1982.

Muller explained that the attorneys within the various fields of tax law belong to a relatively small, almost "cloistered" group, even on a national level. "We have various subcommittees in the American Bar Association," he said, "And those subcommittees are like partnerships. In the 1980s, there was a small group called Civil and Criminal Tax Penalties. These were generally lawyers who did criminal tax defense. That group probably only had about 20 lawyers at the time, although it's grown to be a very large part of the ABA Tax Section." He believed such an intimate number of members allows for much needed communication to take place, with information being disseminated and spread across the country to allow for more effective representation.

Juan enjoyed the deep collegiality and strong friendships that developed between members, and also found that it was not unusual for the attorneys to seek advice from one another about more than the specifics of tax law.

When Juan and Terry attended the Tax Section meeting in Houston, between January 27 and 30, he was happy to greet old friends and make new ones, and always ready to hand out his business cards, but he kept thinking to himself that a judgeship was beyond his reach because he didn't have the right background. "I did not feel qualified to seek the position of a judgeship," Juan said, "I flunked the second grade, and got Ds in high school. Many times I was the lone Hispanic in my classes at UT and felt out of place, and there were many professional rejections after that."

Still, one morning, there was a meeting of the Executive Committee on Tax Court Appointments, and Juan found himself there at 9am. Having been made aware that there was a vacancy on the Tax Court, he stood outside the Oak Room, on the third level of the Westin Galleria & Westin Oaks Hotel.

If there was an opening on the court, he assumed, this must be the location to apply for the position.

"I walked into this small room, looked around to see if I knew anyone," Juan said. "I did not know what to expect. I guess I was expecting to see a table with application forms, which I did not see. Nobody seemed to notice me, so I walked out of the room."

"The court doesn't work that way," explained Terry. "You have to generate your own support to get your foot in the door for consideration. We both learned that a bit later that day."

Indeed, after Juan left the room, he made his way to the main lounge. "I saw my University of Houston professor, mentor, and friend, Ira Shepard. We spoke at length about my feelings for leaving my solo practice, and the pros and cons of seeking a Tax Court judgeship," said Juan. "As we were talking, [Shepard] was getting more excited. He started announcing to nearby attorneys that I was seeking a judgeship to the Tax Court. But I found out that two tax attorneys he introduced me to at that time had previously sought the judgeship and didn't get it. One of them even told me that the process was eight years long and he still didn't get the appointment. My immediate thought was that if these two well-qualified tax attorneys from prominent law firms didn't get the position, what chance did I have?"

Shepard insisted that Juan had a real shot at the judgeship,[1] and the next day he met with Juan and Terry to discuss a strategy. He explained that the President nominates the candidate, but the Senate must approve and confirm the nomination following a recommendation by the Senate Finance Committee. Although each president uses their own procedure for selecting a nominee, President Bill Clinton would rely on a committee of five tax law professionals, working under the Secretary of the Treasury, to find the best candidate.[2]

Emphasizing the point that this was a political appointment and that President Bill Clinton and the Democrats controlled both houses of Congress, Shepard said that Juan being a registered Democrat helped his chances right out of the gate.[3] Additionally, the Secretary of the Treasury was former U.S. Senator from Texas Lloyd Bentsen, who would ultimately recommend the candidates for the president to nominate. Shepard felt that "the stars were aligned" and that this was Juan's "window of opportunity" to get an appointment.

Even with Shepard's optimism, the odds seemed long to Juan—like when he first thought about going to college and later when he was considering law school. But when he and Terry looked back at all they had accomplished together, they decided to take another leap of faith and pursue the judgeship in earnest. That's when the train left the station. It was now a matter of time to see where that train would carry them.

First, they had to get Juan's name in front of the "committee of five" (as the members of the committee to choose a nominee became colloquially known as by Juan and his colleagues involved in his nomination attempt). Shepard recommended that Terry manage a letter-writing campaign intended to generate support from important and influential business and civic leaders in San Antonio, throughout Texas, and beyond. After returning to San Antonio, Terry went part-time with her nursing position, took a desk in Juan's law office, and began sending out letters—hundreds at first, and then thousands (Juan's client list alone counted nearly 1,500)—asking the recipients to consider writing a letter of support for Juan's appointment and sending it to their local congressional representatives, the President, the Secretary of the Treasury, and the members of the committee of five.

Terry also began assembling dossiers on Juan's professional background, including his résumé, biographical information, school transcripts, and copies of the Tax Court cases he worked on, both working for the IRS and in private practice. Everything was neatly contained in blue file folders.

It was hoped that Juan would be considered and eventually confirmed based on his record of achievement and his knowledge of tax law, but it was not lost upon anyone associated with his campaign that to succeed meant Juan would become the first Hispanic in history nominated and confirmed to the U.S. Tax Court.[4] That cultural consideration added an additional sense of obligation to an already important goal.

"It was like a train that we could not stop or get out of, because we had the duty to proceed," said Juan, who continued his solo practice while also making time to speak with as many people as he could about the judgeship.

As Terry continued sending out letters and compiling Juan's dossier, they both wondered if the process would really take eight years. They simply didn't know if they were succeeding or not because neither one of them had any experience undertaking such an endeavor.

One evening in early March 1994, they were both happy to be leaving the office and going out to dinner with their friends Moses and Gloria Berban. The foursome was set to meet at their favorite Chinese restaurant, Taipei.

"In those days, that was the best Chinese restaurant in San Antonio," said Moses Berban, remembering the restaurant from two decades earlier. Berban was a successful businessman, and after Juan did some tax work for him the two eventually became friends, a relationship that extended to Terry and Gloria Berban as well. In addition to recalling his fondness for the food at Taipei, Berban remembered the specific March night when the four met for dinner because of a conversation he'd recently had with Henry B. González, the long-serving U.S. representative from San Antonio. "Henry was very responsive as a congressman. He always stayed in touch with his constituents. He was tough and he always fought for the little guy," said Berban. "And had told me about the need to find a judge for the [Tax Court]."

That conversation was front and center in Berban's mind while waiting on the sidewalk outside the restaurant; he'd already made up his mind that Juan would make an excellent judge.[5] "Juan had compassion when he dealt with people. And he treated his clients with dignity," Berban said. When he asked his wife whether Juan would make a good judge, she agreed that he would.

Later, over dinner, Berban asked if becoming a judge was something Juan had ever thought about.

"We couldn't believe he asked us," said Terry. "We hadn't had the chance to tell him what was going on."

The Vasquezes briefed the Berbans on their undertakings, including the letter-writing campaign. Terry said that a few copies of support letters had arrived in the mail, but there had been no acknowledgment from the White House or the committee of five.

"If it would help, I am meeting with Henry González on Saturday morning, and I could speak with him about your situation," Berban told them.

Without hesitation, Juan thanked his friend for the generous offer.

Although the passage of time has erased what the two couples dined on that night, the evening would prove to be quite fortuitous for Juan. True to his word, Berban told González about Juan. In turn, González asked Berban to send him Juan's résumé, but Berban was ready for the request: "I just so happened to have had it in the car, and I went immediately to retrieve it."

That was about the extent of Berban's interaction with González concerning Juan's judgeship, but it would prove to be as important as having Ira Shepard and Terry working toward the goal. For there was reason to believe that, even though González had nothing to do with the committee nor the Treasury nor, for that matter, the Senate, he was perhaps the best man in the country at that time to be holding Juan's information.

About a week later, on a cold Friday night, Juan was at the office with Terry, finishing some work before leaving for their annual weeklong ski vacation with their sons and some friends. Around 8pm, Jaime, now 12, called from home and spoke to Terry, saying that someone from Washington, D.C., had phoned for Juan. Upon instructions from Terry, Jaime gave the caller the office phone number when he called back. When the office phone rang again, Juan answered the phone and on the other end was the voice of a man named Leslie Samuels, who was the Department of Treasury assistant secretary for tax policy. He introduced himself to Juan and said he was trying to schedule an interview with him in Washington for the next Wednesday to meet with members of the committee considering the appointment to the Tax Court.

"Thank you for your phone call," Juan responded enthusiastically, "but I cannot make it next week because I'm taking my family skiing in Breckenridge, Colorado. Maybe this meeting can be scheduled for the following week?"

On the other end of the phone line, Juan heard Samuels clearing his throat, and it was the kind of clearing that signaled that Juan might not have answered the right way. "It's very difficult to get the committee members together," Samuels said but then added with a bit of mirth, "Washington, D.C. is a beautiful place to visit and bring the family."

During this conversation, Terry had raced to check if Samuels's name was on the committee list. Finding it there, she quickly wrote a note to her husband to "say yes!", which he did immediately, assuring Samuels that he would be there the next Wednesday and adding that his sons "would love learning the history of Washington, D.C."

"After that call, Terry and I looked at each other in amazement. I told Terry that it looked like spring break was going to be in D.C." Juan said.

"We can't take the boys. This is a *working* trip," insisted Terry. After making plans for Juan Jr. and Jaime to stay with family while they were away, Terry called Ira Shepard, who excitedly confirmed Terry's suspicions about how important the meeting was and stressed that Juan needed to be thoroughly prepared because this could be his one shot at the court.

"Ira was a matter-of-fact person and said Juan needed to be strong and persuasive in front of the committee and, at the same time, be his normal self," recalled Terry. "These members were the decision makers who would forward Juan's name to the President if they felt he was qualified."

On Sunday night, March 13, 1994, Juan and Terry flew to Washington to prepare. Letters had been arriving to Juan's office from many people, expressing their support and extolling Juan's track record as an attorney and an active, civic-minded San Antonian. In his letter of support, prominent attorney Frank Herrera Jr. urged the president to consider Juan's appointment, stating that "Juan is an achiever and a conscientious professional who is an expert in tax law," while Antonia Hernández, president and general counsel for the Mexican American Legal Defense and Education Fund, referred to Juan as "eminently qualified for this appointment and would serve our nation with distinction." There was also correspondence from Texas Governor Ann Richards, San Antonio Mayor Nelson Wolff, and high-profile businessman Ruben Munguia. The Hispanic National Bar Association and The Hispanic Bar Association of the District of Columbia threw their support behind Juan. The letters of endorsement were included in the blue folders, ready to present to the committee members.

On Wednesday, March 16, it was very cold. They took a taxi to the Treasury Building on Pennsylvania Avenue. Terry told her husband to have faith and to be strong. "I told him that I loved him and that whatever the outcome, it was all right because we had come this far in a very short time. All was going to be okay," she said.

Terry watched Juan walk up the steps, and then she walked across the street and waited on a bench outside the Old Ebbitt Grill. "I was very nervous. I was wondering how Juan was feeling. Sometimes I paced the sidewalk. Sometimes I prayed," she said.

As Juan climbed the steps to the Treasury, he could see that the building stood next door to the White House, signifying its importance in the nation's business. Inside, he was met by Leslie Samuels, who joked how happy he was that Juan's spring break plans had changed. Samuels took Juan to a large conference room and introduced him to the other members of the committee: Loretta Argrett, Assistant Attorney General, Tax Division, and David Jordan, Acting Chief Counsel, Internal Revenue Service. (Juan had previously met

Jordan when he was a Special Trial Attorney, IRS, out of the Dallas District Counsel office.)[6]

The meeting itself was brief, perhaps 30 minutes. There were the standard interview questions about his background and experience. When asked why he wanted to be a Tax Court judge, Juan explained that he thought it was a logical step for his career as well as a way to be of service to his country. He also learned that there were actually two vacancies on the court at the time. "Then they thanked me for coming in, and while I don't know this for certain, I came away feeling that the gist of the meeting was that they would be glad to consider me for a vacancy in the future. As the meeting ended, I politely thanked them all for their time and gave each one of them a copy of my blue folder for their review," said Juan.

When he met Terry outside, he told her that he felt the meeting had gone well but he felt the reality was that he was possibly being considered for a future vacancy, perhaps next year.

The news did not sit well with Terry. "Next year? We are not waiting for next year," she insisted. Although she wanted to further discuss the meeting, they had another stop to make first. Rita Jaramillo, a liaison to President Bill Clinton, had asked to see Juan after his meeting at the Treasury.[7] So after the short walk, they found themselves inside the White House complex, in the Old Executive Building, where Jaramillo welcomed them. During their brief talk, Jaramillo explained that Representative Henry B. González had written a note on a napkin requesting President Clinton consider Juan as a candidate for the Tax Court. She also mentioned that the congressman had a reputation around Washington for never asking the administration for favors, which made this request a bit of an anomaly and something to be taken seriously.

"Looking back, I think that Congressman González probably wrote that note within a week or so after Moses Berban spoke to him," said Juan. "I'm very grateful for both of their support."

Once back at their hotel, Terry believed they should immediately speak with someone else, perhaps a representative of the Hispanic Caucus, about the current judgeship vacancy. So that afternoon, they walked to the congressional office buildings located about half a mile from their hotel, and found Representative González's contact information on a large silver plaque on the side of the Rayburn House Office Building. They walked to his office on the third floor, and Juan introduced himself and Terry to the legislative aide, explaining that he had just interviewed for the Tax Court judgeship position and wanted to thank González for his support. The aide said the congressman was not available but he would definitely be informed of the visit. They made sure to leave a blue folder for the congressman before leaving.

They also visited some of the offices of representatives of the Hispanic Congressional Caucus, always leaving their greetings and blue folders to pass along with their legislative aides.

The following day they visited the office of Representative Bill Richardson, of New Mexico, who was also chief deputy whip for the House Democrats.

By then they were used to the procedure, and after introducing themselves they handed over a blue folder. This time, however, Juan received an invitation to meet with Representative Richardson later that evening.

"I had a very interesting visit with Congressman Richardson. I educated him about the Tax Court and explained the nomination process," said Juan. "He asked a lot of questions about myself, my tax practice, and my experiences, as well as about the judgeship position."

Back in San Antonio, feeling more determined than ever, Terry continued soliciting letters of support for Juan. About two weeks later, Juan received an invitation to meet with Lloyd Bentsen, Secretary of the Treasury. Again, flights were purchased, sons were cared for, and Juan prepared himself thoroughly for the meeting.

Once again in Washington D.C., Terry waited outside the Old Ebbitt Grill while Juan attended his meeting. Juan immediately noted that Secretary Bentsen's office was a massive room with large windows looking directly at the green lawn of the White House. Bentsen was a tall man with a distinguished demeanor, the same look Juan recognized from seeing him on television and in the newspaper. He spoke with a soft, friendly voice when he asked, "Why do you want to be a judge on the Tax Court?"[8]

It was a question Juan had been asked several times before, and one that he had asked himself many times too. His answer was the same: "I have been a trial lawyer before the Tax Court with the IRS Office of the Chief Counsel for four years and a private attorney for 13 years, and now I want to be in the middle as a judge of the U.S. Tax Court."

Bentsen smiled. They continued talking, and eventually the conversation turned to Juan's early life. "When I spoke to the secretary about my cotton-picking days," Juan remembered, "he told me the story of allowing his son to work in hard labor—digging ditches. When it rained, [Bentsen's son] was happy because he did not have to dig anymore, but his coworker said, 'Don't you understand? If we don't dig, we don't get paid.' This was a valuable lesson he'd learned, and one I learned early in life from my grandfather Jesus Flores."

As the interview ended, Bentsen told Juan that his role in the process was a difficult one because he had been given the names of many qualified candidates. He said that he needed to be something like a "tie-breaking vote" in order to provide the president with a person to nominate. Then he said to Juan, "You will be good for the Tax Court."[9]

Following the meeting with Bentsen, Juan met with Jean Hanson, the general counsel for the Treasury, and Margaret (Peggy) Richardson, the IRS commissioner. Afterwards, he and Terry took a taxi to the airport and returned to San Antonio, satisfied that they had done their best. Then they waited.

Although more copies of letters of support continued to arrive, there was no word from Washington for a month. In a copy of *Tax Notes*, Juan had read a speculative article that mentioned three possible front-runners for the Tax Court vacancies, and he was not on that list. Worse, one of the possibilities was cited as the "only name on the short list culled from the private sector," which implied Juan was not, in fact, being considered for a current vacancy. Then another month passed. Finally, in late June, he received some paperwork to fill out and return to the White House, including background information, school transcripts, résumé, financial information, and more. The FBI first requested further information; then they interviewed the Vasquez's next-door neighbors, and finally interviewed Juan in his office. Ira Shepard assured Juan that this was the normal vetting procedure but cautioned that it didn't ensure the nomination.

Weeks later, the Treasury informed Juan that his name was being submitted to the White House but instructed him to keep the information secret (although he was allowed to tell Terry). He didn't actually know how many other names were being submitted or even if he was being considered for a current vacancy. After all, this was entirely new territory for him, one that included brief, intense moments of activity followed by long periods of anxious waiting.

As summer continued, things remained quiet. There were no more urgent phone calls, no more last-minute D.C. trips, no more juggling of the family's schedules (that is, no more than is normally called for when raising two bright teenage sons). The support mail kept coming in, though, which kept Terry busy at the office. Juan continued his practice and diligently handed out his business cards. At the same time, they couldn't help but wonder if Juan's judgeship journey had met a premature end. Perhaps his name had been dropped from consideration. Perhaps the train had reached the end of the line.

Then on September 6, Representative González called Juan's office. Juan returned the call but missed the congressman and left a message. The congressman called again on September 9 and again missed Juan, who in turn, missed the congressman again. The two never connected. Terry believed the timing of González's call was a positive sign, though. September 15 to October 15 has been recognized as National Hispanic Heritage Month ever since President Ronald Reagan expanded Hispanic Heritage Week, first signed into law by President Lyndon Johnson in 1968, into a month-long observation in 1988.[10] "As September 15 approached, Terry predicted that I would be nominated as a gesture to the Hispanic communities," Juan said. "Sure enough, on September 15, 1994, my cell phone rings and my secretary, Lisa Rodgers, says that Gary Martin, a reporter from *The Washington Post* wanted to get my reaction to being nominated to be the first Hispanic judge on the United States Tax Court. I was shocked in my shoes."

Juan and Terry had been enjoying breakfast at a restaurant close to the office when the call came in. After Juan repeated the news to Terry, he told Rodgers to keep the reporter on the line. They quickly drove to the office, wondering if the news could be true. There had been absolutely no word from the White House or the Treasury. No one had told them anything. Arriving at the office, Terry immediately dialed the operator and asked for the phone number to the White House press secretary's office. Surprisingly, she got through and requested confirmation of Juan's nomination. Within a few minutes, a fax arrived, stating that President Clinton had officially nominated Juan for a current vacancy on the court.

Now the missed call from González made sense. "I strongly believe that the congressman was trying to alert me of this nomination," Juan said. "I am sorry that I did not get the opportunity to speak with him and thank him for his support at that time."

Juan did express his excitement and gratitude about his nomination to the *Post* reporter (who had been on hold for quite some time), and then he called Ira Shepard. His friend and mentor told him how proud and excited he was. He assured Juan that he'd earned the judgeship but that the process was still not over.

Shepard was referring to the hearing with the Senate Committee on Finance followed by a vote from the full Senate to confirm Juan's nomination.[11] Yet in December, when the 103rd Congress ended and all presidential nominations, including Juan's, were returned to the President due to congressional procedures, Juan and Terry wondered if they would have to begin the process again.

As was customary, however, the White House automatically resubmitted the nomination as soon as the 104th Congress convened in January 1995.[12] Juan's confirmation meeting with the Senate Committee on Finance was subsequently scheduled for Thursday, February 16, at the Dirksen Senate Office Building.

It was back to D.C. for another working trip, but Terry and Juan knew this was something else entirely. Juan would be testifying, telling the committee why he was the right person for the job, making his final case, as it were, and doing it in a public forum. Juan Jr. and Jaime, as well as Ira Shepard, made the trip in support.

On Thursday morning, shortly before the hearing, Juan met the other nominee, Maurice Foley, who was there with his wife, Sandy, and their three young children. Foley served as Deputy Tax Legislative Counsel in the Treasury Department's Office of Tax Policy.[13] Foley was also on the precipice of making history: he was poised to become the first African American to become a judge on the Tax Court.[14]

The nominees and their families were escorted to a table in front of a U-shaped desk, at which members of the Senate Committee on Finance were seated. Representative Frank Tejeda, of Texas, introduced Juan, mentioning his work in both the Texas cotton fields and with Western Union while calling attention to his professional achievements. Tejeda said Juan's life had been an "example of excellence in hard work and dedication."

That introduction was followed by a statement from Texas Senator Kay Bailey Hutchison, who echoed Tejeda's support for Juan because of how hard he'd worked his whole life. She said she believed that Juan "really personifies America" and added that she had received letters from her constituents asking her to support his nomination.

When it was Juan's time to testify, he said he was honored to have been nominated. "If confirmed, I will carry out my duties with diligence and fairness," he said. Then, into the Congressional Record, he testified how his work ethic—the one that had brought him to be sitting in front of the Senate Committee on Finance—was the product of his grandparents' example and that, as he became a professional attorney, he "always remembered his grandparents' lesson."[15]

Despite the fact that the hearing lasted only about 30 minutes, Juan thought it was a "nerve-wracking" experience. Afterward, though, he conferred with Foley and decided that the morning had gone well for them both. Terry's letter-writing campaign, suggested by Ira Shepard, had also clearly had an impact on Juan's confirmation process.

Afterward, the family walked to Representative González's office to tell him of the hearing but found he wasn't in. Outside, in the hallway, they turned a corner and saw the congressman. They introduced themselves and updated him about the hearing and thanked him for what he'd done. González smiled, congratulated Juan, and shook the boys' hands. But he apologized that he could not visit long and had to get back to the Capitol.

As the train kept rolling, both nominations were sent to the full Senate, but Juan was not informed of when a vote would take place. The pace of government, he well knew, was usually incremental. He and Terry could only continue with their work, raise their family, and try to wait patiently.

In mid-March, they returned to D.C. for business unrelated to the judgeship journey. But while there, in the afternoon of March 17, Juan's secretary phoned him, excitedly explaining that Maurice Foley had called the office and said that the Senate was taking up the nominations for a vote. When Juan called Foley, he learned that the vote was taking place at that time and Foley was rushing to the Senate Building. In fact, Foley was on hand when the full Senate confirmed them both: History had been made twice, on the same day, for the same court.

It was Friday, March 17, 1995, St. Patrick's Day, when the runaway train finally came to a stop. The journey had taken about fourteen months, even if sometimes it felt like eight years. Juan and Terry had almost reached their destination. Now all Juan had to do was take the oath of office.

CHAPTER NINE

Riding Circuit

In Article 1, Section 8 of the United States Constitution, Congress was given the power to "lay and collect Taxes" in order to, among other functions, "provide for the common Defence and general Welfare of the United States." Known as the Taxing Clause, Section 8 is the authority for all subsequent tax legislation. The clause further allows for Congress to "constitute Tribunals inferior to the supreme Court."

In the first edition of *The United States Tax Court: An Historical Analysis*, written by attorney and Professor Harold Dubroff of Albany Law School and published by the U.S. Tax Court in 1979, the founding of the original body that would become the United States Tax Court is fastidiously chronicled, no easy task considering how many complicated factors led to its creation nearly 100 years ago.

> "As with most institutions, the Tax Court, which was created in 1924 as the Board of Tax Appeals, originated in response to an existing need. In its case the need was created by the combination of two factors. The first of these was the development of the federal income and profits taxes and their emergence during World War I as the preeminent devices for financing the operations of Government. The second was the inadequacy of preexisting institutions, both administrative and judicial, for adjudicating in an acceptable manner the disputes growing out of the changed conditions brought on by the new taxes."[1]

Dubroff's thoroughly researched work shows how the Tax Court needed to continuously evolve as the tax laws and financial circumstances of the country and its need for revenue changed, up to the mid-1970s. The second edition of the book (2015) was undertaken by Professor Brant J. Hellwig, Dean of the

Washington and Lee University School of Law, and clerk for Judge Vasquez from 2000 to 2001; Hellwig's editorial additions address how the court continued changing and expanding its jurisdiction since the circumstances outlined in Dubroff's original release.

Because the Tax Court has been around for so long, *The United States Tax Court* is really the only book that addresses the decades-long bureaucratic, political journey it endured to continue playing a key role in developing a working relationship between this country's citizens and their government. According to *The United States Tax Court*, it proved simply "impossible to draft an income tax statute that clearly provides for all factual circumstances. Accordingly, in addition to the taxing statute, an income tax system requires a sophisticated administrative body to collect the tax and provide interpretations of the statute."

As part of the Revenue Act of 1942, the Board's name was changed to the Tax Court of the United States, and at that time the board members were named as judges. The 1969 Tax Reform Act changed the body's name again, this time to the United States Tax Court. The court does not make tax law but interprets the laws made by Congress and applies those laws to specific cases that come before it.[2] Additionally, as stated in *The United States Tax Court*: "By chartering the United States Tax Court as court of record established under Article 1 of the Constitution through the Tax Reform Act of 1969, Congress supplied the court with a judicial form to match its long-held character as a judicial arbiter."

Cases before the Tax Court are divided into regular and small cases, depending on the amount of money involved. If the amount at issue is $50,000 or less, the taxpayer has the option to have their case filed as a small tax case. If the amount in question is more than $50,000, the taxpayer's case is filed on a regular docket.[3]

When Juan F. Vasquez was confirmed to be a Tax Court judge for a 15-year term, ending in 2010, his role within the realm of law changed again. He needed to learn how to master another job, and that meant that by succeeding in his nomination efforts, which brought the runaway train of his judgeship journey to a halt, it was now time to begin an entirely new phase of his working life.

"We flew home from Washington the day after the confirmation vote. We were happy as can be but didn't know what the next process was to be," Juan remembered, noting that the celebration didn't last too long. For one thing, there was a renewed round of media interest in Juan and his history-making confirmation. He gave interviews to local and national media, including *La Prensa*, which began publishing in 1913 in San Antonio and for a significant length of time was among the most widely circulated Spanish-language newspapers in the country. In the March 24, 1995, edition, reporter Frank Alvarez wrote, "It is obvious that Vasquez enjoys bipartisan support or his nomination would not have survived the changes in the Congress since the November elections." The *San Antonio Express-News* also reported the historic news of Juan's confirmation on March 22 and told readers of his time spent in the cotton fields. Juan also told *Washington Post* reporter Gary Martin, "I'm a firm believer in education. If not for the education I received, I wouldn't be here. It opens doors."

Ever so slowly, as the glare of the media spotlight grew stronger, Juan and Terry began to understand that the parameters of their lives would soon enough be upended.

In early April 1995, the office of the Clerk of the Tax Court called Juan asking for the date of his investiture (the official act of assuming his position) because he was expected—*needed*—in Washington before the end of the month. There was simply no choice but to move forward with a plan to quickly get things in order in San Antonio, including informing his clients of the news, delivering their files, and referring them to other attorneys. With a heavy heart, but also one filled with pride for all he'd accomplished as a private tax attorney, he packed up and then locked the doors to his office, went home, and helped Terry prepare for the move.

Before leaving, there was a going-away party thrown by the Mexican American Bar Association of San Antonio (MABA). The gathering was held at Mi Tierra Café y Panadería, where about 200 people, including family, friends, former clients, and many supporters who had actively backed Juan's journey, celebrated Juan's accomplishment. The artist Jesse Treviño, along with MABA, presented Juan with a sketch of his Fox Tech High School graduation photo, capturing the moment when Juan's future—his current reality—began taking shape.

Juan Jr. and Jaime had grown up seeing their father constantly working, always juggling yellow legal pads, overstuffed file folders, and trial binders. They understood how hard their mother had also worked, both as a nurse and as Juan's number one advocate. As their parents prepared for the move to Washington, they were, of course, living their own lives and taking significant steps toward their own future.

Juan Jr. had moved to Austin and entered the University of Texas a year earlier but still liked to joke that it was his parents who had "broken up the family." Jaime admitted that, being younger, he faced a bit more of an emotional journey. "Girls, sports, games—that's what I was into then, like any kid my age. I was a quarterback. I loved living in San Antonio," he said. "I don't think I was ready for the adjustment to D.C., but it got much better. It turned out to be a unique experience that made me stronger."

Juan and Terry made it to D.C. by the end of April and lived in a simple, furnished, one-bedroom apartment about 30 minutes from Juan's work. It didn't take long for them to find a Washington metro area three-bedroom house with enough room for Jaime (who was staying with relatives while finishing eighth grade and would join his parents in a few months) and just a 15-minute commute from both Jaime's future high school and Juan's office.

It is common for newly confirmed judges to have two investiture ceremonies, a private event to officially begin the judge's term, and a public ceremony to allow family and friends to witness a swearing-in.[4] Juan's private investiture took place on May 1 in the chambers of Chief Judge Lapsley W. Hamblen Jr.[5] Juan was not yet a judge; so he wore a suit and arrived promptly with Terry for the 9am ceremony. He felt humbled as he put his hand on a Bible, held by Terry. Hamblen, who was also dressed in a suit, administered the brief oath of office, by which Juan swore to administer justice "without respect to persons, and do equal right to the poor and to the rich."[6] Afterward, Hamblen said, "Congratulations, Juan. Welcome to the court."

Juan, who had walked into the judge's chambers a private citizen, walked out as the Honorable Judge Juan F. Vasquez of the United States Tax Court. He looked at Terry: they both were in awe of the situation. It had been a collaborative effort to get Juan to this very moment in time, and they had officially made history, yet they still asked one another, "Is this for real?"

It was for real, but there was little time for reflection, much less celebration. That would come later. For now, Juan and Terry headed upstairs to chambers number 17, which formerly belonged to Judge Perry Shields. Now inside Judge Vasquez's chambers, Juan dove right into the job. There were no trials to preside over. That, too, would come later. He first needed to hire the right staff, especially his law clerks to assist him in researching the law, reviewing cases, and formulating opinions. Terry spoke at length with Peggy Tabor, Juan's administrative assistant who had been hired in advance, to review plans for his formal investiture and public ceremony to be held on May 5.

On that day, Cinco de Mayo, the formal investiture took place in the ceremonial center courtroom at the U. S. Tax Court Building. Juan Jr. and Jaime were there. Also present were other Tax Court judges, Ira Shepard, family members from across the country, friends, and various dignitaries, including Judge Kathleen Olivares of the State District Court of Texas, Leslie Samuels, White House representatives Victoria Radd and Rita Jaramillo, former San Antonio councilwoman Mary Alice Cisneros, legislative aides from the House of Representatives and the Senate, and representatives from the IRS and Chief Council Office, the ABA Tax Section, and the Hispanic Bar Association of D.C.[7]

Tax Court Judge Thomas B. Wells, who was an NYU classmate of Juan's, administered the oath of office[8] while Terry again held a Bible for Juan.

After the swearing in, Juan Jr. and Jaime helped their dad put on his official black robe for the first official time. Ira Shepard told the gathered crowd about Juan's upbringing, including his mother's premature passing and his work as a young boy in the Texas cotton fields. Terry's brother Ray Anthony Schultz spoke next about knowing Juan when he was dating his sister while a student at Fox Tech and San Antonio College. Said Schultz, Juan "always had aspirations to better himself."

When the new judge spoke, he said, "To be here this afternoon as a judge of the United States Tax Court is truly an American dream," before thanking a lot of people—from Terry and his sons to his professional colleagues to President Bill Clinton—for the circumstances of the day. He acknowledged those people as his network of support, who had faith in the work he had done so far. "I further commit myself to carry on the worthy traditions of this court and to perform my duties with diligence and fairness. The message to our young people is that with education, persistence, hard work, and love of family and friends, one can reach unimaginable heights."

Although Chad Muller wasn't present at Juan's investiture, he felt quite proud that a San Antonio colleague had been confirmed to such a position. "I think Juan's appointment was a breath of fresh air for the court," he said. "It is absolutely imperative that a Tax Court judge be open-minded and sympathetic to the many taxpayers who didn't really know how to represent themselves at the time of an audit, for instance. They really are frightened. Juan is highly likely to be thorough in getting the taxpayer through the process, and I think that is because of who he is and where he came from. And I don't think he's ever forgotten where he came from."

Other than the Cinco de Mayo fiesta, the first week inside Judge Vasquez's chambers was a busy one. In addition to bringing on another administrative assistant, he was given a small budget to purchase furniture and decor for his office, a task largely undertaken by Terry. He spent time overseeing various administrative tasks, learning how things worked at the court, reading reams of legal paperwork about various cases and the laws he would soon be interpreting, and introducing himself to his colleagues to get their perspectives of the work. (There were 18 other regular judges, plus ten senior judges and ten special trial judges.) He also made it a point to introduce himself to the court building's many staff members.

Though certainly well-versed in tax law and no stranger to the court room, Juan attended an orientation seminar for newly appointed district judges at the Thurgood Marshall Federal Judiciary Building, a program that Tax Court judges are invited to as well. Afterward, Juan met with several other judges on his own to continue his education for conducting trials. In addition to the advice he received to be applied to the courtroom, he was also advised to pack his suitcase efficiently.

That latter advice referred to the fact that the Tax Court is a federal court, which means it hears cases nationwide but with something of a logistical twist. Its judges travel setting up court for certain periods of time in 74 locations around the country.[9] Per Congress, the court provides uniformity to the interpretation of federal tax laws on a nationwide basis, while burdening the taxpayer with as little inconvenience and travel expense as possible in order to argue their case.[10] For the judges, such travel is known as "riding circuit."[11] These travel assignments are made by the chief judge for three sessions per year (fall, winter, spring).[12]

In early June, Juan hit the road, traveling to Los Angeles to observe or "shadow" Senior Judge Irene Scott during one of these trial sessions. This would be the first time that Juan would wear his official black robe while observing from the bench next to Scott.

This would also be the first trip since he and Terry started dating in high school that would take him away for any significant amount of time. "That was not acceptable for us," said Terry. "After all, he did not take this job so that we would be separated. So I did go with Juan on this trip and every single job assignment thereafter for a long, long time." Working part-time as a home health nurse, Terry's schedule could more easily accommodate regular travel assignments than a nursing position in a hospital. "I believe I was the only spouse that traveled regularly because everyone else had other responsibilities, like full-time jobs and young children. Since I am not a government employee, of course, I had to pay for my own expenses."

In Los Angeles, when Judge Vasquez walked into the courtroom with Judge Scott, he noted to himself how the space was packed, wall to wall, standing room only. And it was silent. "They were standing for us and looking at us," said Juan. "During the calendar call, which is the scheduling of the trials for the whole week, the lawyers were extremely respectful." He had never had the opportunity to experience this perspective, from the bench, and he quickly caught on that it was up to the judge, and the judge alone, to control the pace of the proceedings.

As has always been his method, he took copious notes on the trials, as well his observations on the judge's directions to the litigants. Then, as it is to this day, Juan used his unique style of shorthand in his notetaking to quickly and accurately absorb all the information and detail.

After a few days, Judge Scott encouraged Juan to take the gavel (metaphorically, because there is no actual gavel), and Juan selected a real estate deductions trial to preside over. Prior to the trial, scheduled for the next day, he studied the case paperwork, but admitted that as the trial began, he was still nervous because running the proceedings meant bringing another level of confidence to his bearing.

It should be noted that Tax Court judges must be well versed in *all* areas of tax law because specific judges aren't assigned to specific categories of cases, such as corporate tax shelter cases or family limited partnership cases.[13] In 2004, having served on the court for nine years, Juan gave an interview to *The CPA Journal* in which he explained that the calendar of trial sessions can include all types of tax cases. "To borrow a phrase from *Forrest Gump*," he quipped, "each of these calendars is like a box of chocolates—you never know what you're going to get."

In that same article he spelled out how rapidly the court's jurisdiction can grow. "Originally, our jurisdiction was restricted to income, estate, and gift taxes, but Congress has continued to expand our jurisdiction. For instance, in 1996, Congress gave us jurisdiction to hear interest abatement cases; in 1997, worker classification cases; and in 1998, the review of lien and levy cases," he said.

All of which, of course, constitute just a portion of the galaxy of tax cases that are tried in the U.S. Tax Court, including pension, estate, and foreign tax issues.[14] Since many cases involve deciding multiple issues that aren't always resolved in just one party's favor, it was critical for Juan, as a jurist, to retain and retrieve as much information about the specific law germane to the trial at hand, plus whatever trials were approaching on the docket.

Furthermore, there is no jury in these civil tax trials. The judge is the sole arbiter of fact,[15] which means the outcome rests upon the objective assessment of the facts of the case presented during the trial and the interpretation of the law. (Taxpayers who want a jury trial must file a case in the U.S. District Court.)[16] Having practiced tax law for the Office of Chief Counsel and in private practice, Juan knew how the attorneys for the government and the petitioner were attempting to win their cases, and he had to remain a referee, as he came to think of himself, and let nothing but their presentation of the law and the facts persuade his judgment.

U.S. Tax Court Judge David Laro noted the similarities that he and Juan shared after the newest judge on the court found his bearings: "Like Juan, I believe in continuing the work ethic that I had in private practice in my judicial capacity. Also like Juan, I am concerned about the welfare of the ordinary taxpayer and make deliberate efforts to be fair, courteous, and respectful to the participants in trials."[17]

Still, in Los Angeles, taking charge for the first time, Juan was anxious. "I felt a lot of responsibility in hearing the case accurately, getting the facts and letting the witnesses tell their side. I was very concerned that I did the right thing," he said. "After the case, I felt that I had accomplished this goal."

As he already knew, the majority of tax law cases are settled before trial,[18] and the closer the trial date came the more intently the two sides might work to find a compromise. "They get more reasonable. There is a lot of activity on the part of the parties and their attorneys and accountants. The parties begin to see the strengths and weaknesses of their case," Juan said. Due to the fact that a number of cases were settled, the trial calendar did not last the assigned two weeks; so Juan was assigned to shadow Judge Joel Gerber in Reno, Nevada, and then he went to Minneapolis to work alongside Judge Robert P. Ruwe. At both of these trial sessions, Juan was allowed to try cases on his own.

"The true privilege is to watch Judge Vasquez in court," said former Assistant Attorney General of the U.S. Department of Justice Tax Division Kathy Keneally, who is now a partner at Jones Day in New York City. "He shows respect for the lawyers who appear before him, for the government, and for the taxpayers. He is patient and so very thoughtful. No matter the many years that this has been his job, he never forgets that, especially for the taxpayers, this is a new and different experience. The tax law may be complex, and the Court may have rules to follow, but he never loses sight of his core responsibilities as a judge. He strives to make the system not only fair but understandable. He truly serves justice."

For every trial (which are open to the public, by law),[19] Terry sat in the audience. In time, she would witness Juan's confidence grow and know that it was because of how hard he worked to prepare. "I was his unofficial driver," she said. "He studied for the day's cases every day while I drove to court."

Once a trial is concluded, the judge may render a bench opinion at the end of that trial session.[20] In most cases, however, the trial paperwork is sent back to the Tax Court in Washington, where the trial judge and his clerks read through the pleadings, stipulations of facts, exhibits, trial transcripts, judge's notes, and briefs written by the attorneys or pro se (self-represented) taxpayers.[21] The judge and his or her clerks do their own further research of the tax law. Judge Vasquez would confer with his clerks about each case and listen to their input before drafting a report that may become the opinion of the Court.

The Tax Court typically releases two types of opinions: memorandum opinions and Tax Court opinions (or division opinions). A memorandum opinion generally isn't likely to set any precedent because it most often is dealing with a legal issue that has been decided in previous cases, or it narrowly refers to specific facts that are unique to the individual taxpayer of the case.[22] A Tax Court opinion, by contrast, becomes part of the evolution and progression of a specific area of tax law.[23] They include summary decisions[24] for an S case, or small case, which the amount involved for each year is $50,000 or less and in which simplified procedures are used but no right to appeal exists.[25]

In March 2001, the *Houston Business and Tax Law Journal* published a speech by Tax Court Judge Mary Ann Cohen in which she said that, when considering a case and drafting a report, "A judge cannot consider information provided *ex parte* and cannot obtain the advice of a disinterested expert on the law applicable to a proceeding before the judge without giving notice to the parties and affording them the opportunity to respond." Directly addressing "law review authors, commentators and pundits, as well as tax professionals who are using our opinions in their daily work," she cited the Code of Conduct for United States Judges, Canon 3, which states, "a judge should … not be swayed by partisan interests, public clamor, or fear of criticism."

If a report is not sent to the court conference or for court review by the chief judge, the report becomes the opinion of the Tax Court and is released to the petitioner(s) (the taxpayer or taxpayers) and the respondent (the Commissioner of Internal Revenue) of that tax trial, as well as to the public and commercial publishers. If the opinion is a memorandum opinion, or a summary opinion for an S case, the opinion gets published on the Court's website and by private publishers.

If the opinion is a Tax Court opinion, the opinion gets published by the U.S. Printing office in *Reports of the United States Tax Court.* These published opinions are located in each judge's chambers and across the country in law libraries and on the Internet.

"The truly unique aspect of the Tax Court," stated Cohen, "is the statutory prescribed process by which the opinions of the judicial officers are subjected by internal review."

That process is known as the court conference, generally held once a month per the chief judge's decision. Before the court conference, the chief judge circulates the report in question to the court's judges to review.[26] A court conference entails gathering as many regular-status judges that are available to review, discuss, and vote on these reports. Not all judges take part in these conferences because some are traveling for the court. (Each judge typically travels for nine or ten trial sessions per year, returning to Washington in between trips.)[27]

Judges that are in travel status during a court conference can "leave a vote" or vote right after the conference or may decide not to vote.[28]

"It can be like a reunion," Judge Vasquez said about the court conferences. "When we're not traveling, we're often in our offices, working hard. So the conferences are a regular time to see each other."

These conferences are not open to the public nor to the law clerks, respondent, or petitioners. Inside the conference room, next to the chief judge's chambers, there is a long, wide table, with enough seats for the 19 voting judges.[29] There is additional seating for senior judges and the clerk of the court. The chief judge sits on one end, the newest judges sit directly opposite at the other end of the table.[30]

The clerk of the court asks each judge for a yes or no verbal acknowledgment for or against the opinion. The newest judge gets to vote first.[31] "It was nerve-wracking," said Juan. "You don't want to be the first to vote one way and the other 18 judges vote the other way. When I was new to the Court, I had to sit right across the table from the chief judge when I cast my votes."

Court conferences are essentially an internal review of the work done by each judge, similar to the work of an appellate court. "We're sitting in judgment of our colleagues," Juan said, adding that before the voting, the written discussions can at times become tense due to the fact that each judge has put in so much time and energy drafting reports. But Judge Cohen explained of her colleague, "[Juan] brings reasonable viewpoints to the court conference, listens to others, and does not react with anger when others do not accept his position. His temperament is just what the position of Tax Court Judge requires."

If the court conference adopts a report, it is published as an opinion. If it doesn't approve a report, the specific judge who handled the case can agree to rewrite the report and submit it again to the court conference. If that specific judge does not get a majority vote, he or she can also decide to give up the case, the chief judge reassigns it to another judge, and the process starts again until a report is approved. If the new report gets a majority vote, the original judge may decide to write a descent.[32]

Tax Court opinions are appealable to the Court of Appeals that corresponds to the location of the taxpayer's residence or principal place of business.[33]

In addition to taking part in these court conferences, Juan regularly reviewed the current workload with his clerks. Juan preferred discussing matters with his clerks rather than lecturing them about his thoughts of the case.

As he was required to be open-minded during trials, he was always respectful of the opinions from his clerks.

"His patience, willing to listen to others, and understanding of practical impacts to decisions, make him a very effective jurist," said Ivan A. Morales, who served as one of Judge Vasquez's law clerks from 1991 to 2001. "In addition, his good, consistent work ethic instills in others a desire to contribute in a meaningful, positive way."[34]

Another clerk, Jeremy Abrams (2009-2011), said, "Clerking for Judge Vasquez was an incredible experience—he always chats with his clerks in chambers about the docket life and life in general, he introduces his clerks to anyone and everyone he knows (and everyone knows Judge Vasquez!), and he teaches wonderful lessons about tax, life, and how to treat other people."[35]

Over time, Juan would demonstrate that his appointment to the court was not only well deserved but also incredibly beneficial to the institution. Dave Rifkin, who served twice as Judge Vasquez's clerk (1997–1999, 2001–2009), said, "During the period I was at the court, the judge served on almost every standing committee and was asked to chair more than one standing committee. He chaired several task forces that brought about substantial improvement to the internal operations of the court in a wide variety of areas. The judge devoted a substantial amount of time to these endeavors, even if it meant he had substantially more internal work (committee assignments plus task force work) than any other judge."[36]

When the time for his travel grew near, Juan reviewed each trial calendar with his chambers administrator and his two law clerks so that he could adequately prepare. Naturally, he also spoke with Terry, who undertook each trip with him and knew the ups and downs of life on the road. Being a judge in no way exempts someone from the simple reality that occasionally they will be issued the wrong rental car. There might be jet lag and lost luggage. Sometimes, it's impossible to pack for every kind of weather condition. Then there is the inconvenience of traffic and lost hotel reservations, and finding parking and keeping track of every receipt. There is also airport food—*lots* of airport food.

Yet, Juan and Terry had never lacked the desire to see other parts of the country, and they did precisely that for many years in order for him to provide uniform interpretation of the tax laws as mandated by Congress. (Until their youngest son, Jaime, got a little older, whenever it was time for another trip, Juan's aunt and uncle Janie and Jacob Gonzales came to cook and clean and look after their nephew and the Washington area house.) As mentioned earlier, the court holds trial sessions in 74 cities and Judge Vasquez has worked in approximately 60 of these, including Fresno, California; Anchorage, Alaska; Jacksonville, Florida; Portland, Oregon; Salt Lake City, Utah; Dallas, Texas; and dozens of other cities. Washington, D.C., is on the circuit, but Juan has never had trial sessions there. "We prefer not to choose it. We know that many judges have young kids to take care of and other commitments," he explained.

While Judge Vasquez has always taken his job seriously, whether as an attorney or a jurist, there have been a few times of levity in the courtroom, such as when a minister came before him claiming there was nothing in the Code requiring him to file tax returns. When Judge Vasquez urged him to file his returns and the minister refused, he asked, "Don't you want to be a born-again taxpayer?" Despite his stance on taxes, the minister replied, "That's good, Judge."[37]

In July 2010, while addressing the Texas Society of Enrolled Agents in San Antonio, Judge Vasquez recalled a time when he was in the courtroom with Judge Irene Scott.

> At a particular trial session, as [Judge Scott] was scheduling the trials on Monday for the next two weeks, there was a gentleman, the taxpayer, the petitioner in the case—who had previously had his case continued (three or four times)—who informed Judge Scott that he needed another continuance in his case because he was "dying." When this gentleman asked for a continuance, I quickly thought to myself, "What should I do? Should I get down from the bench and help him sit down?" Well, before I could give it a second thought, Judge Scott threw her head back, rolled her eyes, and said, "Oh my heavens! If you are dying, we need to get you to trial right away. We will set your case for trial this Friday—we don't want you to leave a mess for your wife." Well, the case settled that Thursday.

During another trial session, although the IRS lawyer was present, the taxpayer was absent. Judge Vasquez was informed that the IRS was conceding the deficiency and agreeing that the taxpayer owed no additional taxes and was even owed a refund. So why was the taxpayer not present for the proceedings? As Judge Vasquez recalled for his audience in San Antonio, "The government lawyer said, 'He wants us to agree that we will *never* audit him for the rest of his life.'"[38]

While, of course, it wasn't all so amusing, Judge Vasquez's routine would follow a similar pattern of weeks on the road followed by weeks in the office, until May 2010, when his 15-year term ended.

Once again, many professional organizations and individuals rallied to Judge Vasquez's side, taking up the cause to keep him on the court. "The increasing complexity of the tax laws demands the retention and appointment of highly skilled judges to the bench," wrote Charles A. Gonzalez, son of Henry B. González and a former Bexar County District Court judge, who won his father's congressional seat in 1998 following his father's retirement. "I have the highest regard for Judge Vasquez's abilities and am honored to recommend his reappointment to the United States Tax Court."[39]

Judge Vasquez was renominated for another term by President Barack Obama and reconfirmed in October 2011, for another term to end in 2026.[40]

CHAPTER TEN

Legacy

Judge Juan F. Vasquez's chambers in the U.S. Tax Court building is accessed from the fourth-floor hallway through a glass door. Guests enter a warm interior of more than 1,000 square feet. In addition to the reception and administrative assistant area, off to the side there is a small kitchen and a library. There is additional office space for two law clerks, who are also tax lawyers with LL.M. degrees.

Juan's personal office is a very agreeable space, studious and scholarly but balanced by comfort and functionality. Behind the judge's desk there is a large window with a wonderful view of the Statue of Freedom atop the U.S. Capitol building's dome. It's always been a poignant sight for Juan because, as part of his career in tax law, it has been his mission to educate as many people as he can reach that Congress—whose members are working in that Capitol—makes the tax laws, *not* the IRS or its attorneys, and certainly not the judges of the Tax Court. (It has never failed to light a spark inside Juan whenever he has the opportunity to clarify that thorny issue with clients, litigants, and just about anyone else he can pull aside.)

While there is plenty of seating, including several chairs and a dark leather sofa, every available surface is fair game for the judge's work. Tables are usually topped with reams of papers, law books, and file folders, and at times those stacks may make themselves comfortable on the chairs, too. Floor-to-ceiling bookshelves contain copies of *Reports of the United States Tax Court*, hundreds of trial binders, and law books competing for space with keepsakes collected during Juan's travels. There are assorted framed photos of the judge's family as well as of his former clerks, interns, and externs. The mix of personal and professional items reflects a life of intertwining passions and devotions, and when Juan and Terry's grandson once visited, eight-year-old Juan F. Vasquez III ("Juan Tres") called the office "*abuelito's* (grandfather's) museum."

That's not the only moniker that's been bestowed upon these chambers. It's often called the "Jesse Treviño Gallery" by those who've worked or spent much time there because the wall space throughout is devoted almost entirely to the works of Treviño, with whom Juan has continued to be close friends since their first meeting. Among the many framed works is *Los Piscadores*. Alongside it hangs *Viva Fiesta* (2010, acrylic on canvas, 62" × 50"), which was commissioned by Juan F. Vasquez Jr. for his parents' 40th wedding anniversary; it shows the Vasquez family, along with Terry's brother, Ray Anthony Schultz—plus the painting's artist Jesse Treviño himself—watching San Antonio's annual Fiesta Flambeau Parade. The first painting is a reminder of where Juan came from, and the second, a portrait of where he is and what is truly important in his life.

The plethora of Treviño's art did not go unnoticed by the artist himself, who visited Juan's office while he was in Washington in 1997 for the unveiling of Treviño's official portrait of Congressman Henry B. González in the Rayburn House Office Building.[1] "I'm proud that Juan and Terry and their family can stay connected to San Antonio with my art when they are here," Treviño remarked.

It is quite intentional that Juan's office, like his and Terry's D.C.-area home are filled with Treviño's works. As the artist noted, the Vasquezes always find ways to stay connected to San Antonio, which has been very important because Juan has been on the court since May 1995. That means that in 2020, they will have lived 25 years in the Washington D.C. area, longer even than their years working in San Antonio. And while both will acknowledge that when they started the judgeship journey they knew it would take them away from home for several years, neither thought that so much travel away from San Antonio would become their way of life for a quarter century.

Still, having served for so long, Judge Vasquez understands how important it is to not only have a centralized Tax Court in Washington but to also have stability within it. "It's the continuity of the government at work here, with our judges serving from one president to the next without dramatically changing how we operate," he said, quickly adding, "except of course when Congress changes the laws."

In order for the court to have stability, each judge needs stability. Over the years, Judge Vasquez's interns, externs, and various types of law clerks are critical for keeping him updated on the law and especially the current case load he is working on. His office staff, too, must hum with well-oiled efficiency to stay atop of the contemporaneous administrative work that comes with the job. Judge Vasquez has had two chambers administrators during his time on the court: Jean Douglas, who retired in early 2015, and currently Tammy Staples.

"What can I say? Tammy is in charge of division 17 (Judge Vasquez's office)," Terry acknowledges, having spent an enormous amount of time in the office. "She is the timekeeper, the doorkeeper, and the scheduler. She keeps track of all the files and edits the report drafts before they are sent to the chief judge." Like her predecessor, Staples, says Terry, has been integral in helping Juan stay on top of his work and move smoothly through the various phases of his judicial career.

In June 2018, Juan was assigned Senior Judge status. Even though his second 15-year term wasn't set to expire until 2026, by law when he turned 70 he could no longer serve as a regular presidentially appointed full-time judge.[2] Due to the high volume of cases, however, Senior Judge Vasquez continues to be on recall status for the court and regularly rides circuit to help out where needed. He also maintains his office in the Tax Court building.

Since he continues working, Judge Vasquez continues issuing court-affirmed opinions on his cases. As of mid-2020, he had issued 690 opinions.[3] One of those opinions, *Higbee v Commissioner of Internal Revenue*, 116 T.C. 438 (2001), has been cited over 2,150 times, according to LexisNexis.

"His opinions are well thought out and sensible. They are not quirky or cute, but they are the product of hard work and keen intellect. In reviewed cases, he would usually be found on the more correct side of a divided court," said Ira Shepard. Before passing away in March 2016, Shepard had followed Juan's career closely and had taken note of the way he'd conducted himself and how he drafted his reports for the court. "Juan's legacy is that he will be remembered as a solid, well-above-average Tax Court judge."[4]

Despite such an exhaustive record of opinions and decades of hard work, Juan confessed that sometimes when he stops and looks inside his own chambers through the glass door from the hallway, he sometimes feels like a witness to his own life.

"I don't always place myself there when I'm looking in through the door," Juan said, explaining how for a few fleeting moments he can view things with a bit of objective detachment. "But then I *do* recognize that person—me—and I acknowledge he accomplished something. Sometimes, things are better appreciated when you step away from them."

In addition to maintaining his office and continuing to travel for work, Judge Vasquez remains active in numerous organizations such as the ABA Tax Section and the ABA National Conference of Federal Trial Judges. He has also spoken regularly at numerous conferences and functions on matters of importance to tax law and the Tax Court and its legacy, and he has been recognized by many of these organizations for his dedication to the rule of law and for his integrity as a jurist, including by the Hispanic Bar Association of the District of Columbia (which awarded him the Judge Ricardo M. Urbina Lifetime Achievement Award in 2007), the National Association of Enrolled Agents (Outstanding Supporter of EAs Award in 2012), the San Antonio Mexican American Bar Association (Legal Profession Award, 2013), and the Hispanic Bar Association of Houston (Lifetime Achievement Award, 2014).

Juan's peers also recognize the importance of his years of service, and that includes Maurice B. Foley, with whom Juan was originally confirmed to the Tax Court in 1995. "We are tied to each other because we are both very comfortable in our own skin, down-to-earth, and unpretentious," wrote Foley, who was elected by his fellow judges in 2018 for a two-year term as chief judge and re-elected in 2020 for another two-year term. "Among his colleagues, Juan has the biggest heart, and he displays it unabashedly. All litigants (i.e., pro se taxpayers and the proverbial 'little guy') appearing before him are beneficiaries."[5]

Judge Foley's observation of Judge Vasquez's demeanor in court is part of a familiar refrain from other members of the Tax Court bench. In 2014, Chief Judge Howard Dawson Jr. remarked, "We quickly became friends because of his friendly, outgoing, and gracious personality. He was genuine and sincere about become a good, hardworking judge. He was knowledgeable and self-confident, but with no pretense."[6]

Attorney Robert E. McKenzie, of Saul Ewing Arnstein & Lehr LLP, in Chicago, said, "Juan has brought the values he learned from his hardworking family to the bench every day. Anyone lucky enough to litigate before Judge Vasquez realizes that he brings the values of integrity, fairness, and hard work to his job as a Tax Court judge."

When asked about maintaining his many years on the bench with both gravitas and an even temperament, Juan often replies, "God gave me a lot of patience to control my courtroom."

In order to maintain orderly proceedings, though, he must be prepared, and so he must rely on his clerks, to whom he is never shy about giving an appropriately hefty amount of praise. "I've been a success because I've had great law clerks," he said.

When speaking of their memories of working for Judge Vasquez, many former and current law clerks, 28 in total, often state how they learned determination and perseverance from Juan's experiences. "Judge Vasquez's story shows that hard work and positive energy, even (or especially) in the face of great adversity, will lead to personal and professional success. For this and many other lessons, I am thankful and privileged to have Judge Vasquez as a mentor," said Roger Mahon,[7] Juan's current clerk (as of October 2020).

Amy S. Wei, (2001-2003) stated that "among those who know him, [Judge Vasquez] is also one of the nicest judges at the court. He is always happy to meet the new clerks. Also, he is very caring, in that, he always wants to help if he can."[8]

In the courtroom, Judge Vasquez has always concentrated on assisting the parties before him in much the same way he likes to deal with his clerks. In other words, he spends as much time listening to and understanding any problems and concerns before proceeding in an authoritative manner.

"I am in the unique position of being the judge's first law clerk to have served as his trial clerk," said Ben Friedman (2012-2014). "[Judge Vasquez] treats all taxpayers fairly and with respect. He is very accommodating to both parties in a case. He is very calm on the bench. He took a lot of time to study up on the facts and law of the case before the trial and during the trial so that he would be prepared on the bench."[9]

Because Juan has always been diligent about working closely with his clerks, during the interview process he seeks an initial connection on which they might build a solid relationship. Having been the first and the only alumni of the University of Houston Law Center to be a Tax Court judge, Juan's proclivity has been to hire clerks from the University of Houston as well as from New York University. But wherever he finds his clerks, his work with them has been instrumental in their continued success. "They've all gone on to do very well," said Juan, noting that his former clerks currently work in prestigious law firms across the country as well as for the Internal Revenue Service, the Justice Department, and several prominent accounting firms.

In turn, his clerks' views on their former boss are universally positive and respectful. Brant Hellwig, who clerked from 2000-2001 and is now Dean of the School of Law at Washington and Lee University and who also wrote the second edition of the *United States Tax Court: An Historical Analysis*, said, "The legacy of Judge Vasquez has many facets. Perhaps the most obvious is that he was the first Hispanic judge of the court. He also rose to the court from an austere upbringing, as reflected in the Jesse Treviño painting [*Los Piscadores*]. In my view, however, his legacy is that a solo practitioner specializing in tax controversy work ended up being appointed to the Tax Court bench. In that respect, Judge Vasquez brought a different perspective to the Tax Court."[10]

Juan has always been quick to acknowledge the help he has received in his life and in turn has deliberately sought out opportunities to share his experience and knowledge with others, which doesn't just include law students or colleagues. "Juan seldom turns down an opportunity to speak to children, Hispanic bar groups, and community organizations," wrote Chief Judge Maurice Foley. "Indeed, he joined Special Trial Judge John Dean and me in founding and running a mentoring group for underprivileged elementary school children. Once a month Juan, John, and I would drive to Silver Spring, Maryland, to meet in a conference room with a small group of troubled fourth and fifth graders."[11]

As mentioned before, Juan has always displayed the quality of understanding, with clients, litigants, other attorneys, and people he meets in everyday life. Before being confirmed as the 49th Commissioner of Internal Revenue in 2018, Charles "Chuck" Rettig worked for 36 years as a tax attorney at Hochman, Salkin, Rettig, Toscher & Perez, P.C.,in Beverly Hills. While working as an attorney, he noticed Juan's down-to-earth approach to life and respected how it guided his work. "Juan appreciates the realities and practical aspects of life," Rettig stated. "Few outside the tax world would know he is a federal judge, but all would receive a warm welcome and an invitation to sit and 'talk story,' as though he didn't have a plane to catch, an opinion to write, transcripts to review, et cetera. He makes time for others and has a genuine interest in *their* story, *their* life, and *their* experiences. He has long served as an inspiration to myself, my family, and numerous others."[12]

Without a doubt, Juan also served as an inspiration for his sons, Juan Jr. and Jaime. Since both grew up observing their father ascending the career ladder and expressing his fulfillment with the climb, it is not surprising that they both have built similarly successful and gratifying lives.

After high school, Jaime Vasquez received his bachelor's (2003) and master's (2004) degrees in accounting from the McIntire School of Commerce at the University of Virginia. He worked as a CPA and immensely enjoyed the field. He noted that his father was always supportive of him, no matter which path he intended to take. "My brother and my dad wanted me to go straight to law school. I wanted to give the CPA thing a chance. I had a knack for it. My dad was really good about all my choices, even when I rejected the idea of initially going to law school. He didn't pressure me. He would have been happy if I was an engineer or if I went to medical school."

Jaime did return to school, getting a J.D. in 2008 from the University of Texas School of Law and an LL.M. in Taxation from the New York University School of Law in 2009. He is currently a shareholder at Chamberlain Hrdlicka in San Antonio. "Now, I'm kind of doing the same thing my dad did 25 years ago, when he was practicing in San Antonio, representing taxpayers with disputes with the IRS."

Jaime's wife, Veronica Vasquez is a Bexar County Probate Court Judge; they have one child, Daniella.

Chad Muller, who works with Jaime Vasquez at Chamberlain Hrdlicka, said he sees similarities between father and son. "I see the same philosophy in Jaime of wanting to really help people. Of course, he wants to make money and feed his family, but he's much more willing to take a small case because the taxpayer is struggling."

Juan Jr. started out as a liberal arts major at the University of Texas in Austin and then went into the McCombs School of Business. "My dad got into the UT business school, and I saw the importance of business and accounting in his life and profession," said Juan Jr. "I fondly remember coordinating with my tax accounting class professor to have my dad speak to the class as a UT accounting graduate and sitting Tax Court judge. I remember being impressed with my dad, the court, and his position and the history behind all of it. It actually helped guide me toward tax and, really, the family profession."

After getting his B.B.A. in 1998, he received his J.D. (2001) from the University of Houston Law Center and his LL.M. in Taxation (2002) from the New York University School of Law. He is a shareholder at Chamberlain Hrdlicka in Houston. He is also an adjunct professor at the University of Houston Law Center, where he teaches, alongside his father, a class on tax controversy and litigation.

"I thought it would be a great way to spend time with my dad if we were both teaching together, and it would be a way to give back to the university that had done so much for both of us," said Juan Jr. "A lot of tax classes are focused on the tax planning side; this class focuses on the tax controversy side. The students really enjoy him as a professor and as a person. I'm crazy impressed with my dad being able to cite relevant code sections, and the students love the war stories from his years working as a government attorney, a private practice attorney, and a federal tax court judge."

Juan Jr. is married to Lindsey Vasquez; they have four children, Claire Amelia, Maryn Graciela, Juan III, and Lauren Olivia.

Having two sons in the tax law profession is an immensely gratifying aspect of life as a parent for Juan, who said, "I certainly consider our sons and what they've accomplished as tax attorneys to be a part of my legacy."

For a quarter century, Juan has traveled the country interpreting the rule of law for the American taxpayers. At each stop on the circuit, Terry has served as his unofficial assistant, driver, and confidant, which has granted her the unique perspective of seeing him at work over the course of many years.

"Being in the courtroom gives me much satisfaction as I see and hear Juan in action," said Terry. "Being there has taught me what his job was all about, and I learned much more about his position and the responsibility that comes with it. I felt happy for our culture and for our families' many generations that my Juan would become a judge and do such a wonderful job. It was fulfilling not only for me as a wife but for regular people like ourselves."

There was a time, however, when Terry had to discontinue accompanying Juan for work. "I traveled with Juan until my mother, Mary Ruth Schultz, got ill. She began showing signs and symptoms of Alzheimer's disease, and I moved back to San Antonio in 1998 to take care of her," she said. Terry's mother had started being very forgetful as far back as 1996, and her other troubling symptoms continued to progress and worsen over the years, which included after the passing of Terry's father, Reyes G. Schultz, in 1998.

The separation was hard on both Terry and Juan. Juan often put in 10- to 12-hour workdays at his D.C. office or in the temporary courtrooms set up on the road until the time arrived each week for him to fly back to San Antonio. In Terry's 2008 memoir, *Mi Mamacita Tiene Alzheimer's* (*My Beloved Mother Has Alzheimer's*), she writes about the times when Juan returned home to San Antonio to visit us. "That was fun and most rewarding to us all! It was like a cheerful welcoming. The weekends were very different for all of us. We did special things together. We went to church, breakfast, all meals, [took] drives and special trips. My husband and I made weekends special for *mi mamacita* and us."

After so many years of being a nurse and caring for strangers, taking care of her own mother, who passed away on February 17, 2012, was still a challenge. But it opened her eyes to the many problems of degenerative brain diseases for both patients and caregivers and for years she has undertaken Alzheimer's advocacy work. Despite the extra travel, despite the difficulty of taking care of someone suffering from a major disease, Juan said it was his and Terry's duty to take care of family as they did, but they did not see it as a disheartening undertaking. "We did not consider it a burden. We did it because it was the right thing to do," Juan said. "There was no question that I would help out as much as I could during that time. I wanted to be there for the family."

When reflecting upon his work as a Tax Court judge, Juan has previously stated, "Sometimes, things are better appreciated when you step away from them." His thoughts also ring true about home, and home for Juan and Terry will always be San Antonio. For in addition to being the first Hispanic confirmed to the Tax Court, Juan was also the first San Antonian to wear the robes for that institution as well. (Judge Elizabeth Copeland, appointed in 2018, was born in Colorado, but prior to her judgeship she practiced law in San Antonio for 23 years.)[13]

At Mi Tierra, in San Antonio's historic and vibrant Mercado District, the celebration on November 14, 2014, to illuminate Juan's portrait within *American Dream* would prove to be one of the most fulfilling days Juan and Terry have experienced—this after a lifetime of fulfilling days. There on the wall were images of Representative Joaquin Castro and his brother, former San Antonio mayor and HUD Secretary Julián Castro, prominent local lawyer Frank Herrera, beloved Tejano singer Selena Quintanilla, legendary West Side printer Ruben Munguia, and well-known businesswoman and staunch supporter of San Antonio's arts and cultural institutions Rosemary Kowalski, among so many others.

When the spotlight shone onto the newly painted image of Juan in his judge's robes—also revealing a miniature depiction of *Los Piscadores* behind him—Juan knew he was in very good company. In their own ways, almost each person in the mural has made it a mission to ensure San Antonio is a wonderful place to call home while extending their mission to enrich Hispanic and Latino populations throughout San Antonio, the country, and beyond. The mural has essentially become a wall of fame for local, national, and international personalities, and despite his humility at the scope of his life and career, Juan's presence lends even more importance to the enormous, colorful work of art. As Juan has said, "When your hometown honors you, it's special."

"It has been an honor and a privilege to serve my country, including the great state of Texas," Juan said, adding, "I see pride and perseverance in each of the portraits. The people on this mural each represent hard work, endurance, humility, and family with the Hispanic and Latino communities. Without a doubt, being added to the *American Dream* mural has been one of the wonderful experiences of my life."

It should not go without saying that Juan had a lot of help along the way, and at the center of that help, since his senior year in high school, has been Terry. After Juan had been confirmed to the court, Moses Berban (who passed away in 2019) remarked about Juan's success in this manner: "Juan's grandfather and Terry did the most to help shape Juan's life. Terry has truly been very important in helping Juan get his success." Berban was not the first nor the last to assert that, alongside her husband, Terry also has pursued and achieved the American Dream, with all the hardships and challenges and victories that come with the undertaking.

Judge Mary Ann Cohen, who believed Juan to be an "excellent and compassionate judge as well as a tax scholar," also mentioned, "I know [Juan] and Terry are an inseparable partnership, sharing everything from meals to spectacular travel adventures."[14]

Chad Muller stated, "I've never known any woman who has been more supportive of her husband—and her boys—than Terry. She went to bat for him to get his appointment, she travels with him, and she enjoys that role. I've never seen that level of dedication."

"Terry has been so central and is the foundation of our entire success," Juan said. "Meeting Terry redirected my entire life and future plans, and it's undeniable that she played the crucial part in my seeking a Tax Court nomination and the whole historic journey."

"It had to do with growing together, since we met in high school. Everything out in the world was new. We were young and adventurous. We were willing to be open-minded about opportunities that would come in," Terry said to William D. Elliott in the video feature "Texas Tax Legends" in October 2017. "Our goals kept changing, but we talked about it. That's part of mutual respect."

With Terry's support, Juan has risen to life's challenges again and again by displaying the same dedication to hard work that he was taught by his grandfather Jesus Flores. It's what he brought to his telegram-delivery job, sometimes pedaling his bicycle beyond what he thought was possible. It's what he eventually took to his education, bearing down in his classes to forge ahead and make a better life for his family. It's what his employers discovered he would always bring to his work, and it was what his thousands of clients in private practice came to count on.

Such professionalism is why so many colleagues like Antonio Mendoza, former associate professor at Pepperdine University, initially urged President Clinton to nominate Juan for a judgeship by writing, "[Juan Vasquez's] grasp of the issues, his fairness, his judiciousness, his strict adherence to the highest ethical standards and his vast knowledge of the tax law impressed me greatly. He possesses a deep technical knowledge of the law and is blessed with good common sense. As a CPA, tax lawyer, and now tax professor, I can unequivocally say that Juan clearly stands out among his peers."[15]

Once confirmed to the United States Tax Court, the Honorable Judge Juan F. Vasquez committed himself to learning as much as he could about the laws he was interpreting while earning a reputation as an empathetic jurist to the parties who came before him. Accompanied by the legacy of the court, he has established himself as a widely respected judge.

And it all started in the cotton fields of South Texas.

Los Piscadores remains important and inspirational to Juan, although he doesn't have to look at the painting to be reminded of his humble roots. He carries with him the memories of his family working hard while Apa Flores calls out, '*Sume la bota!*'"

"It was among the best bits of knowledge he passed along," remembered Juan. "Do your best and be the best, no matter what you do."

AFTERWORD

Reflections on Picking Cotton

It's understandable that many people find the fact that I picked cotton to be one of the more interesting parts of my journey. It's a way of life now long gone. Although it has negative connotations in some communities, it never fails to bring to mind the idea of backbreaking work and a strong will to endure. It built character. It taught lessons, lessons that I still consider important and relevant up to this very day.

But back in 1955, when I started living with my mom, I was roundly deterred. The cotton crew leader and truck driver, Don Trini, would always come and pick up families from San Antonio; my uncles, aunts, and cousins had picked cotton for years, and the kids always made it sound like it was fun, just like going on a trip. So I remember asking my mom why we couldn't go. She told me she didn't want us to pick cotton because she knew how hard it was.

After she died and I moved into my Flores grandparent's home, in 1957, I would soon learn who was telling the truth about picking cotton. That first summer, being in the intense heat, feeling like I was going to faint, seeing snakes and spiders, I realized what my mom meant. In the fields, my tennis shoes were almost of no use. The soil got so hot that my feet felt like they were burning. It took that first year to understand how dangerous the work was.

The last year I picked cotton was 1963. I was 14 before I got to the cotton fields, and by the time we'd packed up and left for the year, I was 15. I had become a pretty good picker. In the beginning I would have picked no more than 50 pounds a day. By the end I was picking 600 pounds a day. Word got around about who could pick the most pounds in a day. There was a certain pride in being the best cotton pickers in the camp, and I wanted to be known as a good cotton picker.

More importantly, we—the Flores family—took a lot of pride in being part of my grandfather's team. We had a good reputation among the other workers. That mattered because of the 15-20 families that Don Trini picked every year to go to Taft, maybe four or five of them returned the next summer. There would be new pickers at the camp every year, while we kept returning, proving that we were reliable.

Away from the fields, though, perceptions were different. Other segments of the society, including the Hispanic society, looked down on such labor. I don't recall telling a lot of people when I was young about picking cotton. I really can't remember, but we *might* have been embarrassed that we were cotton pickers. At the start of the school year, we would get new blue jeans and a shirt for James Fannin Elementary School, and the kids would make fun of me because they knew the money for the clothes came from picking cotton.

Over the years I've met people who've told me that they picked cotton, but it was just for a summer, or maybe a week, sometimes just a day. One summer, my next-door neighbor on Montana Street named Futsy wanted to join us picking cotton. He took a bus to Taft on a Saturday. On Monday he went to work in the fields. He was light-skinned, and the sun was so hard on him. He turned red, and I thought he was going to have a heart attack. By ten in the morning, he was underneath the truck, hiding from the sun. He only lasted half a day.

Cotton picking is not for everybody, but that's hardly an issue today. The country has moved on from manually picking cotton, something my grandfather foresaw happening in the early 1960s. The harvesting machines displaced hundreds, maybe thousands of workers in the fields, which reminds me of the headlines today warning of robots taking away more and more jobs across all industries. I guess that's progress.

I never really looked at it like this before, but I'm of the last generation that picked cotton by hand. To some extent I'm glad we're not going back to the cotton fields because it was grueling work, but we also learned something about character, especially from my Grandfather Flores, always encouraging us to do our best. And later in life, I discovered that other people I admired picked cotton. When I read Audie Murphy's autobiography *To Hell and Back*, I learned his Texas family were sharecrop farmers and raised cotton. Murphy was one of the most decorated combat soldiers in World War II and then went on to have a career in Hollywood. As a child Johnny Cash picked cotton on his family's Arkansas farm, and he became one of the most successful performers in the world.

Recently I learned about Army Master Sergeant Roy Benavidez, born in Cuero, Texas, and orphaned by the time he was nine. He was raised on a sharecrop farm and picked cotton until he was 19, when he joined the army. Benavidez served in Korea and Vietnam, where he earned five Purple Hearts and became a Green Beret. In 1981, President Ronald Reagan presented him with the Medal of Honor.

Hearing about these and others who started out life toiling in the fields makes me proud of my past. I feel like we share the same ethic of enduring hard work, the same one I took with me to deliver telegrams. We cotton pickers also understood a simple but important lesson, one that I teach to my clerks, staff, sons, and grandchildren: Doing more gets you more. The more cotton we picked the more money we got paid. The more I studied, the more my grades improved. I saw the results in the fields by getting paid every Saturday morning, and I saw results in the classroom by going from Ds to As.

Today, the more work I put into my cases—to the point of knowing the cases as well as both sides before me know their cases—the better judge I become. I learned that lesson in the cotton fields with my grandfather, Don Jesus Flores. I hope I can pass that along—by example—to future generations. *¡Sume la bota!*

—Juan F. Vasquez

Special Acknowledgment

Muchas, muchas gracias to my coauthor, Anthony Head. Thank you from the bottom of my heart for helping to bring to life this incredible story of the first Hispanic judge appointed to the United States Tax Court, who is also my husband.

During the past several years, while we collaborated, I learned many lessons from you. I've also appreciated your wit, your soothing tone when things got tough, your creativity, your inspiration, and your determination to see this through to the last page.

Sume la bota,
Mary Theresa Vasquez

Acknowledgments

From Mary Theresa Vasquez

First and foremost, thank you to my dear Lord for giving me the health, inspiration, patience, and guidance to coauthor this biography and for guiding me to my coauthor, Anthony Head, for helping me in accomplishing this mission.

Special thank you to my parents, Mary Ruth Montez Schultz and Reyes Gonzales Schultz, for their love, strength, and guidance throughout my life.

Special thank you to Juan's mother, Amelia Flores Vasquez and his paternal and maternal grandparents, Don Jesus and Basilia Flores and Juan Reyes and Victoria Resendez Vasquez, for their love and support in raising an honest and loving son.

Most special thank you to my beloved husband of 50 years, Juan F. Vasquez. Also special thanks to my two sons, Juan F. Vasquez Jr. and Jaime Vasquez and their wives, Lindsey Vasquez and Veronica Vasquez, and all my beloved grandchildren, Claire Amelia, Maryn Graciela, Juan F. Vasquez, III (Juan Tres), Lauren Olivia, and Daniella Vasquez and Viviana Vasquez (due to be born in late November 2020), as well as my former daughter-in-law, Alison Vasquez.

Thank you to all of my siblings for their love and support during this journey and most especially to my brother, Ray Anthony "Tony" Schultz, for his many hours of technical support and his beloved words, and additionally his wife, Tinker, for her love and support. And to all our extended families, Montez, Schultz, Flores, and Vasquez, and most especially José Vasquez Jr. ("Uncle Jr."), his sister Sylvia Berlanga and his brother Raymundo Flores Vasquez, who passed away on March 29, 2018.

Thank you to our many friends, current and former, in our beloved hometown of San Antonio, Texas, and across our nation as well as in the Washington, D.C. area, and to those who have passed away, including Gloria and Moses Berban and Dr. Ariel Hernandez Jr. from San Antonio, Texas.

Very special thank you to all our dear friends who wrote letters of support for this manuscript.

Special thank you to my dear friend and educator, Belinda Arredondo, who contributed the inspiration for the this book's discussion guide as well as Jennifer Velasquez, teen services coordinator of the Teen Library at the San Antonio Central Library for book clubs and students. Additionally, to my former daughter-in-law, Alison Vasquez, and my granddaughter, Claire Amelia Vasquez, whom helped me formulate some of the discussion guide questions as well as the Wondermom Wannabe website (https//wondermom-wannabe.com/book-club-questions) for its guidance.

Special thanks to the former President William Jefferson Clinton and the former President Barack Obama for their nomination of Juan F. Vasquez as a judge to the U.S. Tax Court and to the nomination committee staff, as well as the Senate Finance committee staff, which helped during this historical nomination process.

Special thank you to all who wrote letters of support for the judicial journey: from Juan's former law firm clients, former employment colleagues and educational institutions, which include elementary, junior high, high school, San Antonio college, University of Texas, State University of New York in Buffalo, University of Houston Law Center, and New York University, and most especially to professor and mentor Ira Shepard from the University of Houston Law Center.

Thank you to all former and current congressional representatives, senators, all civic and other organizations for their support of the tax court judgeship/journey/process.

Thanks to all the U.S. Tax Court staff who came into Juan's everyday work life and offered their support. Special thanks to the U.S. Tax Court judges/colleagues who contributed letters of support of their thoughts on Juan's legacy, including former Chief Judge Howard Dawson, former Judge David Laro, former Chief Judge Mary Ann Cohen, and current Chief Judge Maurice Foley.

Special thanks to Juan's former chambers administrator Jean Douglas and secretaries Peggy Tabor and Angie Grow, and the almost thirty administrative attorney advisors and over seventy Interns/Externs in assisting me in this biography.

Very, very special thank you to Juan's current chambers administrator, Tammy Staples, and Roger Mahon, administrative attorney advisor, for their endless support to me in making this biography a success.

To all former clients, friends, and acquaintances through lifetime, all alumni schools, as well as professional friends and all civic organizations, thank you.

Special thanks to the ABA Tax Section for publication of this book. We hope that this book demonstrates to all children that to succeed in life one must "*Sume la bota.*"

We're both extremely grateful to Todd Reitzel for his enthusiasm for the project as well as his skills as an editor. Thank you also to him and to Gregory Peacock for giving the book its lovely look. And to everyone at the American Bar Association Tax Section, we say, gracias!

Anthony would like to express his fondness to Terry, Juan, and Anthony's wife, Michele, for all the fun involved with the project.

Most special thanks to all those whose names may have been missed above.

Endnotes

Chapter One

1. History of Mexican quarter: author interview with Henry Cisneros (former mayor of San Antonio).

2. History of Mi Tierra: author interview with Jorge Cortez (owner, Mi Tierra).

Chapter Two

1. Letter from Amelia Flores: collection of Juan F. Vasquez

Chapter Three

1. Migration from Mexico to Texas for agriculture jobs: https://tshaonline.org/handbook/online/articles/npt01; accessed April 12, 2018.

Chapter Four

1. Speaking Spanish not allowed in San Antonio public schools: author interview with Joe Bernal (former San Antonio teacher, state legislator).

2. Fox Tech history: https://www.mysanantonio.com/life/life_columnists/paula_allen/article/Paula-Allen-Fox-Tech-occupies-site-of-S-A-s-795718.php; accessed November 11, 2018.

3. Use of teletype machines, Western Union: https://westernunion-westernunion.blogspot.com/; accessed October 21, 2018.

4. "James H. Meredith, who set out to show Mississippi Negroes…": from original teletype, June 6, 1966; collection of Juan F. Vasquez.
5. *Life* magazine published photos of Meredith seconds after getting shot: *Life*, June 17, 1966, page 30.
6. Civil rights luminaries take up Meredith's action: https://www.smithsonianmag.com/history/down-in-mississippi-85827990; accessed October 30, 2018.
7. Juan worked alongside White House Press Corps at Tropicano: Foster, Ed. "Press Corps Invades S.A.." *San Antonio Light*, March 6, 1966, page 5-A.
8. On Christmas Eve, President Johnson visited Kelly Air Force Base; https://www.britishpathe.com/video/president-johnson-welcomes-vietnam-wounded; accessed July 2, 2018.

Chapter Six

1. Minorities tended to be placed on audits of municipalities; author interview with Juan F. Vasquez.
2. There was little chance to get assigned the audit of, say, a big automaker: author interview with Juan F. Vasquez.
3. Being an African American in this era: author interview with Juan F. Vasquez.
4. Basic rights for minorities had been legislated by congress and upheld by the Supreme Court: https://constitution.laws.com/the-supreme-court/civil-rights; accessed March 28, 2018.
5. Judges for the United States Tax Court…travel to Houston about eight to ten times a year: author interview with Juan F. Vasquez
6. In private practice, the attorney for the taxpayer might only have one case per session: author interview with Juan F. Vasquez
7. Of the hundreds and hundreds of lawyers working for the Chief Counsel's office …a handful were Hispanic: author interview with Juan F. Vasquez.

Chapter Seven

1. Treviño was a famous artist: Head, Anthony. *Spirit: The Life and Art of Jesse Treviño*, Texas A&M University Press, 2019.

2. Information on Juan and Jesse Treviño, including family and business relations: author interview with Juan F. and Terry Vasquez.

3. Treviño wanted $9,000 for *Guadalupe & Calaveras*: author interview with Juan F. and Terry Vasquez.

4. *Los Piscadores* was loaned to "Chicano Visions" tour: author interview with Juan F. and Terry Vasquez; Marin, Cheech. *Chicano Visions: American Painters on the Verge*, Bullfinch, 2002.

5. Juan and Terry wanted to keep an eye on their painting; author interview with Juan F. and Terry Vasquez.

6. Marin often gave personal tours of the exhibition: author interview with Juan F. and Terry Vasquez; https://www.ocala.com/news/20060128/traveling-exhibit-portrays-chicano-art; accessed December 3, 2013.

7. The 6.7 magnitude Northridge earthquake: https://www.history.com/topics/natural-disasters-and-environment/1994-northridge-earthquake; accessed February 1, 2019.

Chapter Eight

1. Shepard insisted that Juan had a real shot at the judgeship; author interview with Juan F. and Terry Vasquez.

2. Although each president uses their own procedure for selecting a nominee, President Bill Clinton would rely on a committee of five tax law professionals...: author interview with Juan F. and Terry Vasquez.

3. Shepard said that Juan being a registered Democrat helped his chances: author interview with Juan F. and Terry Vasquez.

4. Juan would become the first Hispanic nominated and confirmed to the U.S. Tax Court: Martin, Gary. "Alamo City lawyer becomes first Hispanic on Tax Court." *San Antonio Express-News*, page 12A.

5. Berban already made up his mind that Juan would make an excellent judge: author interview with Moses Berban.

6. Samuels took Juan to a large conference room and introduced him to the other members of the committee: author interview with Juan F. Vasquez.

7. Jaramillo explained that González had written a note on a napkin requesting President Clinton consider Juan as a candidate: author interview with Juan F. and Terry Vasquez.

8. Information on Secretary of the Treasury Lloyd Bentsen: https://www.britannica.com/biography/Lloyd-Bentsen; accessed on January 3, 2019.

9. Bentsen told Juan that his role in the process was a difficult one: author interview with Juan F. Vasquez.

10. September 15 to October 15 recognized as National Hispanic Heritage Month: https://www.hispanicheritagemonth.gov/about/; accessed on July 3, 2018.

11. Shepard was referring to the hearing with the Senate Committee on Finance: author interview with Juan F. Vasquez.

12. The White House automatically re-submitted the nomination…: interview with Juan F. and Terry Vasquez.

13. Foley served as Deputy Tax Legislative Counsel in the Treasury Department's office of Tax Policy: https://www.taxnotes.com/imp/17169716; accessed August 2, 2016.

14. Foley was poised to become the first African American on the Tax Court: https://www2.law.temple.edu/10q/chief-judge-maurice-foley-of-the-u-s-tax-court-fall-2019-fogel-lecture/; accessed September 1, 2020.

15. Juan's statement to Senate: copy of speech, collection of Juan F. Vasquez.

Chapter Nine

1. "As with most institutions, the Tax Court…": Dubroff, Harold, Hellwig, Brant J. *U.S. Tax Court, An Historical Analysis*, page 1.

2. Information on history of Tax Court, including name changes: Dubroff, Harold, Hellwig, Brant J. *U.S. Tax Court, An Historical Analysis*, pages 13, 172, 175, 186, 236.

3. Cases before the Tax Court are divided into regular and small cases: https://ustaxcourt.gov/about.htm; accessed March 12, 2019.

4. It is common for newly confirmed judges to have two investiture ceremonies: author interview with Juan F. Vasquez.

5. Information on Hamblen: author interview with Juan F. Vasquez.

6. Oath of office: copy of oath, collection of Juan F. Vasquez.

7. Information on second investiture ceremony, including guests and quotations: *Tax Court Newsletter*, Spring 1995, Number 42.

8. Judge Thomas B. Wells administered the oath of office: *Tax Court Newsletter*, Spring 1995, Number 42.

9. Tax Court is made up of traveling judges: https://ustaxcourt.gov/taxpayer_info_about.htm; accessed March 12, 2019.

10. The Court provides uniformity to the interpretation of federal tax laws: Dubroff, Harold, Hellwig, Brant J. *U.S. Tax Court, An Historical Analysis*, page 755.

11. Riding circuit: https://www.fjc.gov/history/timeline/circuit-riding; accessed March 13, 2019.

12. Travel assignments are made by the chief judge: Tidrick, Donald. "In Focus: Inside the U.S. Tax Court." *The CPA Journal*, January 2004.

13. Specific judges aren't assigned to specific categories of cases: "ABA Tax Bridge to Practice Series," speech by Judge Juan F. Vasquez, collection of Juan F. Vasquez.

14. U.S. Tax Court cases include pension, estate, and foreign tax issues: Tidrick, Donald. "In Focus: Inside the U.S. Tax Court." *The CPA Journal*, January 2004.

15. While conducting civil tax trials there is no jury: "arbiter of fact," https://www.ustaxcourt.gov/taxpayer_info_glossary.htm#TRIER_OF_FACT; accessed April 13, 2019.

16. Taxpayers who want a jury trial must file a case in the U.S. District Court: https://www.irs.gov/irm/part9/irm_09-006-004; accessed January 13, 2019.

17. "Like Juan, I believe in continuing the work ethic…": letter from Judge David Laro, collection of Juan F. Vasquez.

18. The majority of tax law cases are settled before trial: https://ustaxcourt.gov/about.htm; accessed February 21, 2019.

19. Tax Court trials are open to the public by law: Dubroff, Harold, Hellwig, Brant J. *U.S. Tax Court, An Historical Analysis*, pages 69. 94, 112, 454.

20. Once a trial is concluded, the judge may render a bench opinion: "Rule 152. Oral Findings of Fact or Opinion." United States Tax Court Rules of Practice and Procedure, https://www.ustaxcourt.gov/rules.htm; accessed May 12, 2019.

21. In most cases, trial paperwork is sent back to the Tax Court for opinions: author interview with Juan F. Vasquez.

22. Memorandum opinion: https://www.ustaxcourt.gov/taxpayer_info_after.htm; accessed March 20, 2019.

23. Tax Court opinion or division opinion: "Tax Court Opinion or Memorandum Opinion," https://www.ustaxcourt.gov/taxpayer_info_after.htm; accessed March 20, 2019.

24. Summary opinion: https://www.taxcontroversy360.com/2016/10/types-of-tax-court-opinions-and-their-precedential-effect/; accessed March 20, 2019.

25. "S" case: https://www.ustaxcourt.gov/taxpayer_info_glossary.htm#SMALL_TAX_CASE; accessed March 21, 2019.

26. Before court conference, the chief judge circulates the report for review: Dubroff, Harold, Hellwig, Brant J. *U.S. Tax Court, An Historical Analysis*, page 759.

27. Judges typically travel for nine or ten trial sessions per year: interview with Juan F. Vasquez.

28. Not all judges take part in court conference: author interview with Juan F. Vasquez.

29. 19 voting judges in court conference: https://ustaxcourt.gov/about.htm; accessed April 22, 2019.

30. Information about court conferences, including seating: author interview with Juan F. Vasquez.

31. Court conference voting details: author interview with Juan F. Vasquez.

32. If the court conference adopts a report, it is published as an opinion. If it doesn't...: Dubroff, Harold, Hellwig, Brant J. *U.S. Tax Court, An Historical Analysis*, pages 759-760.

33. Tax Court opinions are appealable to the court of appeals: https://www.ustaxcourt.gov/taxpayer_info_after.htm#AFTER6; accessed March 25, 2019.

34. "His patience, willing to listen to others...": letter from Ivan A. Morales, collection of Juan F. Vasquez.

35. "Clerking for Judge Vasquez was an incredible experience...": letter from Jeremy Abrams, collection of Juan F. Vasquez.

36. "During the period I was at the Court...": letter from David Rifkin, collection of Juan F. Vasquez.

37. Trial session with minister: "A Little Bit of Tax Humor" speech by Juan Vasquez, July 8, 2010, collection of Juan F. Vasquez.

38. Trial session with IRS conceding to taxpayer: "A Little Bit of Tax Humor" speech by Juan Vasquez, July 8, 2010, collection of Juan F. Vasquez.

39. "The increasing complexity of the tax laws…": Letter from Charles A. Gonzalez, collection of Juan F. Vasquez.

40. Renominated for another term by President Barack Obama: https://ustaxcourt.gov/judges/vasquez.htm; accessed February 17, 2019.

Chapter Ten

41. 1997 unveiling of Treviño's portrait of Congressman Henry B. González in the Rayburn House Office Building: email from Felicia Wivchar, February 8, 2016.

42. By law, when he turned 70 he could no longer serve as a regular presidentially appointed full-time judge: Dubroff, Harold, Hellwig, Brant J. *U.S. Tax Court, An Historical Analysis*, page 217.

43. As of mid-2019, Juan has issued 690 opinions: data supplied by Juan F. Vasquez.

44. "His opinions are well thought out and sensible…": email from Ira Shepard to Terry Vasquez.

45. "We are tied to each other because we are both very comfortable…": letter from Judge Maurice Foley, collection of Juan F. Vasquez.

46. "We quickly became friends because of his friendly…": letter from Judge Howard Dawson, collection of Juan F. Vasquez.

47. "Judge Vasquez's story shows that hard work and positive energy…": letter from Roger Mahon, collection of Juan F. Vasquez.

48. "Among those who know him…": letter from Amy S. Wei, collection of Juan F. Vasquez.

49. "I am in the unique position of being the judge's first law clerk to have served as his trial clerk…": letter from Ben Friedman, collection of Juan F. Vasquez.

50. "The legacy of Judge Vasquez has many facets…": letter from Brant Hellwig, collection of Juan F. Vasquez.

51. "Juan seldom turns down an opportunity to speak to children…": letter from Judge Maurice Foley, collection of Juan F. Vasquez.

52. "Juan appreciates the realities and practical aspects of life…": letter from Charles "Chuck" Rettig, collection of Juan F. Vasquez.

53. Information on Judge Elizabeth Copeland: https://obamawhitehouse.archives.gov/the-press-office/2015/05/01/president-obama-nominates-elizabeth-ann-copeland-united-states-tax-court; https://www.ustaxcourt.gov/judges.html.

54. "Excellent and compassionate judge as well as a tax scholar…": letter from Judge Mary Ann Cohen, collection of Juan F. Vasquez.

55. "[Juan Vasquez's] grasp of the issues, his fairness, his judiciousness…": letter from Antonio Mendoza, collection of Juan F. Vasquez.

Sources

Interviews

Juan and Terry Vasquez were interviewed in person approximately a dozen times between January 31, 2012, and August 20, 2019. Additionally, there were several phone interviews and dozens of email exchanges.

The following persons were interviewed by phone, unless otherwise indicated.

Moses Berban

Joe Bernal

Georgina Cardenas

Henry Cisneros, in San Antonio

Jorge Cortez, in San Antonio

Paul Dostart

Joyce Dostart

Adolph Flores

Kathy Keneally

Leonard Krzywosinski

Robert E. McKenzie

Chad Muller

Martin Press

Ray Anthony Schultz

Jesse Treviño, in San Antonio

Jaime Vasquez

José Vasquez Jr.

Juan Vasquez Jr.

Periodicals

The CPA Journal

Houston Business and Tax Law Journal

Life

La Prensa

San Antonio Express-News

San Antonio Light

Tax Court Newsletter

Books

Dubroff, Harold, and Hellwig, Brant J. *U.S. Tax Court, An Historical Analysis.* U.S. Tax Court, 2015.

Flynn, Jean. *Henry B. Gonzalez: Rebel with a Cause.* Eakin Press, 2004.

Head, Anthony. *Spirit: The Life and Art of Jesse Treviño.* Texas A&M University Press, 2019.

Marin, Cheech. *Chicano Visions: American Painters on the Verge.* Bullfinch, 2002.

Peña, Manuel. *Where the Ox Does Not Plow: A Mexican American Ballad.* University of New Mexico Press, 2008.

Rosales, Rodolfo. *The Illusion of Inclusion: The Untold Political Story of San Antonio.* University of Texas Press, Austin, 2000.

Vasquez, Mary Theresa. *Mi Mamacita Tiene Alzheimer's.* Vantage, 2008.

Web Resources

"1994 Northridge earthquake." https://www.history.com/topics/natural-disasters-and-environment/1994-northridge-earthquake.

"About National Hispanic Heritage Month." https://www.hispanicheritagemonth.gov/about/.

Allen, Paula. "Fox Tech occupies site of S.A.'s first high school." https://www.mysanantonio.com/life/life_columnists/paula_allen/article/Paula-Allen-Fox-Tech-occupies-site-of-S-A-s-795718.php.

"Biography," "How do I file an appeal from the Judge's decision? Can I appeal my case?," "Judges," "Life Cycle of a Tax Court Case," "Rule 152. Oral Findings of Fact or Opinion," "Rules of Practice and Procedure," "Small Tax Case (S Case)," "Tax Court Opinion or Memorandum Opinion," "Trier of Fact," "What is the United States Tax Court?" https://ustaxcourt.gov.

Butler, Carolyn. "Down in Mississippi." https://www.smithsonianmag.com/history/down-in-mississippi-85827990.

Brown, Norman. "Texas in the 1920s," Henderson, John. "Sanatorium, TX." Texas State Historical Association, https://tshaonline.org.

"Civil Rights Act of 1964." https://constitution.laws.com/the-supreme-court/civil-rights.

"Circuit Riding." https://www.fjc.gov/history/timeline/circuit-riding.

"Elizabeth Ann Copeland." https://obamawhitehouse.archives.gov/the-press-office/2015/05/01/president-obama-nominates-elizabeth-ann-copeland-united-states-tax-court; https://www.ustaxcourt.gov/judges.html

"Gross, Foley, Saunders on Tax Court Short List." https://www.taxnotes.com/imp/17169716.

"History." https://westernunion-westernunion.blogspot.com/.

"Lloyd Bentsen: American Politician." https://www.britannica.com/biography/Lloyd-Bentsen.

"Maurice B. Foley." https://www2.law.temple.edu/10q/chief-judge-maurice-foley-of-the-u-s-tax-court-fall-2019-fogel-lecture/; accessed September 1, 2020

"Part 9. Criminal Investigation. Chapter 6. Trial and Court Related Activities. Section 4. Trial." https://www.irs.gov/irm/part9/irm_09-006-004.

"President Johnson Welcomes Vietnam Wounded 1966." https://www.britishpathe.com/video/president-johnson-welcomes-vietnam-wounded.

Roberson, Andrew, and Spencer, Kevin. "Types of Tax Court Opinions and Their Precedential Effect." https://www.taxcontroversy360.com/2016/10/types-of-tax-court-opinions-and-their-precedential-effect/.

"Texas Tax Legends." State Bar of Texas, Tax Section, interview by William Elliott, October 2017. http://www.texastaxsection.org/; accessed June 18 2019.

Wittenauer, Cheryl. "Traveling exhibit portrays Chicano art." https://www.ocala.com/news/20060128/traveling-exhibit-portrays-chicano-art.

Appendixes

U.S. Tax Court Committees on Which Judge Vasquez Has Served

1995–2006: Admissions, Ethics, and Discipline

1999, 2001, 2007: Judicial Conference

2000–2002: Building, Court Facilities and Court Security

2000–2004: Rules

2004–2006: Legislation

2004–2007: Human Resources

2006: Chair, Travel Regulations Study Group

2006–2008: Budget

2006–2008: Training and Development

2008: Chair, Training and Development

2008–2010: Chair, Admissions, Ethics, and Discipline

February 2015: Employee Dispute Resolution; Pro Se Taxpayers

August 2015 – present: ABA Judicial Division; Executive Committee National Conference of Federal Trial Judges

August 2016: Employee Dispute Resolution; Pro Se Taxpayers/LITC

July 2018 – July 2020: Chair, Employee Dispute Resolution

July 2018 – July 2020: Co-Chair, Outreach

July 2018 – July 2020: Pro Se Taxpayers

List of Judge Juan F. Vasquez Opinions by Year

Year	Division	Memorandum	Summary	Bench	Dissent	Concurrence	Total
1995	1	1	0	0	0	0	2
1996	0	13	1	1	0	0	15
1997	1	21	0	0	0	0	22
1998	0	23	0	1	0	0	24
1999	4	19	0	0	0	0	23
2000	7	16	0	0	1	0	24
2001	8	19	0	0	1	1	29
2002	6	25	1	0	1	0	33
2003	4	28	2	0	0	3	37
2004	2	28	0	0	0	0	30
2005	0	26	0	0	0	0	26
2006	5	21	0	0	4	0	30
2007	1	86	3	0	1	0	91
2008	2	50	11	0	0	1	64
2009	1	26	2	0	0	0	29
2010	1	18	3	1	0	0	23
2011	0	21	3	5	0	0	29
2012	1	23	1	6	0	0	31
2013	1	16	6	0	0	0	23
2014	2	13	1	1	1	1	19
2015	0	13	1	0	0	0	14
2016	1	12	7	0	0	0	20
2017	0	18	2	0	0	0	20
2018	0	13	0	0	0	0	13
2019	0	9	2	0	0	0	11
2020	0	8	0	0	0	0	8
Total	48	566	46	15	9	6	690

Juan F. Vasquez Awards and Recognitions

1988

"Certificate of Merit", Pro Bono Law Project of Bexar County Legal Aid, San Antonio, Texas

1989–1990

"Sembradores Education Foundation Corporate Sponsorship Award", Sembradores de Amistad, San Antonio, Texas

1990–1991

"Meritorious Service Award, In recognition of your contributions as a member of the IRS/Practitioners Liaison Committee", Austin District, Internal Revenue Service

1991

"Outstanding Member Award", Mexican American Bar Association, San Antonio Chapter

"President's Service Award", Mexican American Bar Association, San Antonio Chapter, San Antonio, Texas

1992

"Mentor to Junior High School Students Award", Mexican American Bar Association, San Antonio Chapter, San Antonio, Texas

1993

"South Side YMCA Sponsor Award", San Antonio, Texas

"Mentor to Junior High School Students Award", Mexican American Bar Association, San Antonio Chapter, San Antonio, Texas

1995

The Mexican American Bar Association—Recipient of "Recognition of Your Support & Dedication to Our Organization"

1996

"Outstanding Member Award", Mexican American Bar Association, San Antonio Chapter

2000

San Antonio Bar Foundation—Life Fellow, In Recognition of Devotion & Commitment to the Bar

2005

National Association of CPAs of Mexico (Colegio Contadores Publicos de Mexico), Acapulco, Mexico

Washburn University School of Law, Business & Transactional Law Center—Recipient of Distinguished Tax Law Visitor, Topeka, Kansas

2006

The University of Houston Law Center (UHLC) Alumni Snapshot: Honorable Juan F. Vasquez by James West Dullar, Houston, Texas

2007

ACPEN, Tax Controversy Toolkit—Recipient of "In Recognition of Your Contribution to the Continuing Education of CPAs"

The Hispanic Bar Association of the District of Columbia—Recipient of the Judge Ricardo M. Urbina Lifetime Achievement Award, Washington, D.C.

2012

National Association of Enrolled Agents National Conference—Outstanding Supporter of Enrolled Agents Award, Las Vegas, Nevada

2013

San Antonio Mexican American Bar Association—Legal Profession Award, San Antonio, Texas

2014

Hispanic Bar Association of Houston—Lifetime Achievement Award, Houston, Texas

State Bar of Texas Convention, Section of Taxation—2014 Outstanding Texas Tax Lawyer Award, Austin, Texas

Recognition into the Latino Legacy—The American Dream Wall, Mi Tierra Restaurant, San Antonio, Texas

2015

Hispanic National Bar Association—Annual Uvaldo Herrera Moot Court Competition, San Antonio, Texas

2018

Endowed Establishment Scholarship of the Honorable Juan F. Vasquez, U.S. Tax Court Judge, University of Houston Law Center, Houston, Texas

Speeches Given by Judge Vasquez

1995

October 17: Detroit Bar Association, Detroit, MI

1996

January 30: San Francisco Tax Litigation, San Francisco, CA

June 17: L.A. Association of Tax Counsel, Los Angeles, CA

November 18: St. Louis Metro Tax Bar Association, St. Louis, MO

1997

February 13: HBA of the District of Columbia, "Remarks Regarding U.S. Tax Court Clerkships and Internships", Washington, D.C.

March 18: Capital University Law School, Columbus, OH

June 12: San Francisco Tax Litigation Club, San Francisco, CA

September 23: Hispanic Heritage Awards, Dallas, TX

1998

February 2: Pepperdine University School of Law, Malibu, CA

February 23: L.A. Association of Tax Counsel, Los Angeles, CA

April 8: Federal Judicial Center, Program for Judges from Argentina, "The Operations of the U.S. Tax Court", Washington, D.C.

April 16: University of Texas, College of Business Administration, Austin, TX

September 30: University of Texas at Austin, Graduate Program, "Remarks on the U.S. Tax Court", Austin, TX

October 14: San Francisco Tax Litigation Club, San Francisco, CA

1999

January 15: ABA, Section of Taxation Midyear Meeting, Panelist, "Tax Court Jurisdiction Over Employment Tax Disputes—Good or Bad?", Orlando, FL

September 22-24: National Judicial College with the participation of Supreme Commercial Court of the RF, Sponsored by USAID, "Comparative Analysis of the Settlement of Disputes Arising From Tax, Customs, and Other Administrative Matters", Moscow, Russia

September 28-30: National Judicial College with the participation of Supreme Commercial Court of the RF, Sponsored by USAID, "Comparative Analysis of the Settlement of Disputes Arising From Tax, Customs, and Other Administrative Matters", Khabarovsk, Russia

November 1: L.A. Association of Tax Counsel, Los Angeles, CA

2000

March 5-10: National Institute for Trial Advocacy (NITA), Notre Dame Law School, Instructor, "Litigating Before the U.S. Tax Court", Denver, CO

March 20: L.A. Association of Tax Counsel, Los Angeles, CA

March 24: Pepperdine University School of Law, Malibu, CA

August 29: National Association of Enrolled Agents, Washington, D.C.

October 1: Howard University School of Law, Dean's Lecture Series, Speech on Career Path, Washington, D.C.

October 17: San Francisco Tax Litigation Club, San Francisco, CA

November 8: University of Houston Law Center, 2nd Annual Corporate & Taxation Law Society, Panelist, "Presenting Your Best Case to the Tax Court", Houston, TX

December 6: Nova Southeastern University Law Center, Ft. Lauderdale, FL

December 7: South Florida Tax Litigation Association, Miami, FL

December 8: The Greater Ft. Lauderdale Tax Council, "Practicing in the Tax Court", Ft. Lauderdale, FL

2001

January 12: ABA, Section of Taxation Midyear Meeting, Panelist, "Tax Court Jurisdiction in Worker Classification Disputes Revisited; Recent Trends in Collection Due Process Cases", Scottsdale, AZ

February 6: Southern Methodist University, Graduate Tax Program, Dallas, TX

March 27: Cleveland Bar Association, "Remarks from the U.S. Tax Court", Cleveland, OH

April 18–20: U.S. Tax Court Judicial Conference, Panelist, Charlottesville, VA

June 5: Texas Society of CPAs, 8th Annual Forum, Dallas Chapter, Panelist, "A Panel Discussion on the United States Tax Court", Dallas, TX

July 19: Federal Bar Association, Taxation Section, Panelist, "Career Opportunities in Tax Law for Young Tax Lawyers and Summer Associates", Washington, D.C.

September 22: Texas Society of Enrolled Agents, Austin, TX

October 29: Wayne State University Law School, "The U.S. Tax Court", Detroit, MI

November 20: San Antonio Estate Planners Council, San Antonio, TX

2002

January 22: Texas Society of CPAs, Houston Chapter, Panelist, "Tax Controversies: Where We've Been and Where We're Going", Houston, TX

February 11: Mississippi Bar Association, Tax Section, Jackson, MS

April 18: Chemonics International, Inc., USAID grant, Judicial Reform Project in Morocco, Commercial Court of Agadir, "Introduction to the U.S. Tax Court", Washington, D.C.

April 19: University of Virginia, McIntire School of Commerce, Speech and Field Trip to the United States Tax Court, Washington, D.C.

September 23: L.A. Association of Tax Counsel, Los Angeles, CA

November 8: 50th Annual Tax Conference, University of Texas School of Law, "Trends in the Tax Court", Austin, TX

2003

January 24: ABA, Section of Taxation, Midyear Meeting, "Tax Court Proceedings Under Seal, Practical Issues", San Antonio, TX

January 27: Arkansas Bar Association, Tax Section, Little Rock, AR

February 26: L.A. County Bar Association, Taxation Section, "The Do's and Don'ts of Tax Court Practice", Los Angeles, CA

May 9: ABA, Boston, MA

June 11: Arizona State Bar Annual Convention, Tax Section, Panelist, "Tax Disputes from Cradle to Grave", Phoenix, AZ

September 12: ABA, Section of Taxation and Section of Real Property Probate and Trust Law, Joint Fall CLE Meeting, Panelist, "Ethical Obligations in Disclosing Computational Errors", Chicago, IL

October 17: University of Virginia, Business School, "The U.S. Tax Court", Charlottesville, VA

November 15: Texas Society of Enrolled Agents, Speech & Tax Court Mock Trial, Galveston, TX

2004

January 12: L.A. Association of Tax Counsel, Los Angeles, CA

May 26: San Francisco Tax Litigation Club, San Francisco, CA

August 24: NYU, "The Tax Court's Law Clerk (Attorney-Adviser) Program", New York, NY

October 27: Greater Denver Tax Counsel Association, "The U.S. Tax Court", Denver, CO

2005

January 6: Texas Society of CPAs, Houston Chapter, Tax Expo, Houston, TX

March 10: National Association of CPAs of Mexico (Colegio Contadores Públicos de México), Acapulco, Mexico

May 17: 12th Annual Tax Alliance Conference, University of Texas at Dallas, "Tax Court Mock Trial", Richardson, TX

October 19: HNBA Convention, Panelist, "Tax Court Litigation and Income Tax Treaty Application", Washington, D.C.

October 27: Washburn University School of Law, Topeka, KS

November 30: San Francisco Bar Association, Section of Taxation, "Remarks from the U.S. Tax Court", San Francisco, CA

2006

February 27: L.A. Association of Tax Counsel, Los Angeles, CA

March 9: Greater Orange County Bar Association, Tax Section, "Remarks from the U.S. Tax Court", Los Angeles, CA

March 31: University of Florida Law School, Graduate Tax Program, "Perspectives from the Bench", Gainesville, FL

May 9: Portland Tax Bar Association, Section of Taxation, "Remarks from the Tax Court", Portland, OR

July 14: Texas Society of Enrolled Agents, Speech & Tax Court Mock Trial, Waco, TX

October 16: L.A. Association of Tax Counsel, Los Angeles, CA

November 1: 43rd Annual Hawaii Tax Institute, Chaminade University Tax Foundation, Panelist, "The United States Tax Court", Honolulu, HI

November 16: Greater Ft. Lauderdale Tax Council, Miami, FL

2007

February 28: Utah State Bar, Tax Section, "The Do's and Don'ts of Tax Court Practice", Salt Lake City, UT

March 28: State Bar of Michigan, Taxation Section, "Views from the Tax Court", Detroit, MI

April 18–20: U.S. Tax Court Judicial Conference, Williamsburg, VA

May 15: Hillsborough County Bar Association, Tax Section, "Views from the Tax Court", Tampa, FL

June 22: State Bar of Texas Convention, Tax Section, "Views from the Tax Court", San Antonio, TX (2 panels)

October 17: Business Professionals' Network Inc., Accounting CPE, (ACPEN), Panelist, "Going to the Tax Court", Dallas, TX

October 20: NY State Society of Enrolled Agents, Speech & Tax Court Mock Trial, Albany, NY

November 9: Hispanic Bar Association of DC (Awardee)

November 27: University of Texas Tech School of Law, Lubbock, TX

2008

January 28: L.A. Association of Tax Counsel, Los Angeles, CA

March 6: Howard University Law School, "Introduction to the U.S. Tax Court", Washington, D.C.

April 10: University of Houston Law Center, Business & Tax Law Journal, Keynote Speaker, Houston, TX

June 19: 15th Annual Tax Alliance Conference, Panelist, "The Do's and Don'ts of Tax Court Practice", Dallas, TX

October 19: NYU's 67th Institute on Federal Taxation, Panelist, "Strategies and Techniques in Civil and Criminal Tax Controversy and Tax Litigation", New York, NY

November 9: NYU, 67th Institute on Federal Taxation, Panelist, "Strategies and Techniques in Civil and Criminal Tax Controversy and Tax Litigation", San Diego, CA

December 1: L.A. Association of Tax Counsel, Los Angeles, CA

2009

January 9: ABA, Section of Taxation, Midyear Meeting, "A Discussion of Diversity in Tax Law", New Orleans, LA

January 9: ABA, Section of Taxation, Young Lawyers Forum, Law Student Tax Challenge, Panelist, New Orleans, LA

January 14: Federal Bar Association, San Antonio Chapter, "An Overview of the United States Tax Court, Current Significant Legal Developments and Do's and Don'ts of Tax Court Practice", San Antonio, TX

March 19: State Bar of Michigan Tax Section, Detroit, MI

March 31: Tax Executives Institute, 59th Midyear Conference, "The State of Tax Litigation in the United States & Canada: A View from the Bench", Washington, D.C.

April 29: Arizona State Bar Tax Section, "The Do's and Don'ts of Tax Court Practice", Phoenix, AZ

June 12: NYU, 1st Annual Tax Controversy Forum, Panelist "Judging Your Case: Perspectives from the Bench", New York, NY

August 20: Hawaii Society of Enrolled Agents (Mock Trial), Honolulu, HI

September 8: U.S. Dept. of Justice, Dallas Bar Assoc. Tax Section, Dallas, TX

October 7: Gonzaga Law School, Spokane, WA

October 24-26: NY State Society of Enrolled Agents, 22nd Annual Convention, Albany, NY

November 30: Association of Tax Counsel, Los Angeles, CA

2010

January 21–23: ABA, Section of Taxation Midyear Meeting, San Antonio, TX

March 10: Hostos Community College, Bronx, NY

May 5: Tax Attorneys from Bay Area, San Francisco, CA

June 17: Tax Court Panel, 17th Annual Tax Alliance Conference, Plano, TX

July 8: Texas Society of Enrolled Agents, State Convention, San Antonio, TX

December 8: Low Income Tax Clinic Conference, Washington, D.C

2011

January 10: LSU Law Center, New Orleans, LA (dinner w/students)

January 12: Louisiana State Bar Association Tax Section, New Orleans, LA

January 20-22: ABA, Section of Taxation Midyear Meeting, Boca Raton, FL

February 8: Portland Tax Bar, Portland, OR

March 8: North Carolina Tax Section, Winston-Salem, NC

August 7–9: National Association of Enrolled Agents Conference (Mock Trial), Las Vegas, NV

August 19: Advance Tax Law Course Panel, Houston, TX

September 14: Young Tax Lawyers of the State Bar of CA Taxation Section, San Diego, CA

October 18: Washington State Society of Enrolled Agents (Mock Trial), Seattle, WA

October 20–22: ABA, Section of Taxation, Denver, CO

December 13: Arizona State Bar, Phoenix, AZ

2012

February 18: ABA, Section of Taxation Midyear Meeting, San Diego, CA

March 5: NY County Lawyers' Association, New York, NY

April 18: Utah State Bar, Tax Section, Salt Lake City, UT

August 24: Hispanic National Bar Association, Seattle, WA

2013

January 25: Countdown to Reform: Creating an Internal Revenue Code that Reflects

America, ABA, Section of Taxation Midyear Meeting, Orlando, FL

May 9–11: ABA, Section of Taxation, Washington, D.C. (Awardee)

June 17: L.A. Association of Tax Counsel, Los Angeles, CA

June 28: Washington State Society of Enrolled Agents, State Convention, Marysville, WA

September 6: Hispanic National Bar Association, Denver, CO

September 20: U.S. Russia Foundation for Economic Advancement & the Rule-of-Law, Vladivostok and Moscow, Russia

November 18: Idaho University Law School, Boise, ID

December 4–6: University of Texas Tax Conference, Austin, TX (Awardee)

2014

January 23–25: ABA, Section of Taxation Midyear Meeting, Phoenix, AZ

May 8–9: Hispanic Bar Assoc. of Houston, Houston, TX (Awardee)

June 4–6: ABA, Section of Taxation, Miami, FL

June 25–27: State Bar of Texas Convention, Tax Section (Awardee)

July 6: Texas Society of Enrolled Agents, State Convention (Mock Trial), San Antonio, TX

July 17: Washington Society of Enrolled Agents, Tacoma, WA

September 11: HNBA Annual Convention, Washington, D.C.

September 18–20: ABA, Section of Taxation, Joint CLE Meeting, Panelist, Denver, CO

October 15: New Jersey Society of Enrolled Agents, Cranbury, NJ

November 3: SMU, Dallas, TX

December 10–12: ABA, National Institute on Criminal Tax Fraud & Tax Controversy, Las Vegas, NV

2015

January 29–31: ABA, Section of Taxation Midyear Meeting, Houston, TX

March 27: Fredric G. Levin College of Law, University of Florida, Gainesville, FL

May 22: Tax Court Judicial Conference, Durham, NC

June 3: Florida Bar Taxation, Tampa, FL

August 1–2: ABA Annual Meeting, Panelist, Chicago, IL

August 2–4: National Association of Enrolled Agents Convention (Speech & Mock Trial), Las Vegas, NV

September 16: CA Bar Association Tax Section (BAYTL), San Francisco, CA

November 17: Howard Law School, Washington, D.C.

2016

January 28–30: ABA Midyear Meeting, Section of Taxation, Los Angeles, CA

April 5: Federal Bar Association Section on Taxation, Law Day Program for Eastern High School, Washington, D.C.

April 11: Idaho State Bar, Tax Section, Boise, ID

May 18: Connecticut State Bar, Tax Section, CPAs & Enrolled Agents, Hartford, CT

September 20: Indianapolis State Bar Association, Tax Section, Indianapolis, IN

September 29 – October 1: ABA, Section of Taxation, Joint CLE Meeting (Judge Dawson speech), Boston, MA

November 29: Federal Bar Tax Section, Dallas, TX

December 7–9: ABA, National Institute on Criminal Tax Fraud & Tax Controversy, Las Vegas, NV

2017

January 19–21: ABA, Section of Taxation Midyear Meeting, Orlando, FL

January 20: ABA Midyear JD Panel, Orlando, FL

March 23: Beverly Hills Bar Association, Los Angeles, CA

April 12: San Francisco Bay Area, San Francisco, CA

April 20: "OMG, I Have a Case in the U.S. Tax Court," panelist, live webinar, ABA Judicial Division & ABA Center for Professional Division

May 5: Florida State Bar, Tax Section, Palm Beach, FL

July 17: HBNA Internship Luncheon Program

September 14–15: ABA Joint CLE Meeting, Young Lawyer's Forum & Diversity, Austin, TX

September 26: NYC Taxpayer Advocate, Gibson Dunn, New York, NY

December 6–8: ABA, National Institute on Criminal Tax Fraud & Tax Controversy, Las Vegas, NV

2018

June 5: 25th Annual Tax Alliance Conference (Mock Trial), Plano, TX

August 1: "Education and Diversity," panelist, ABA Judicial Division Standing Committee on Diversity in the Judiciary, junior and high school students selected from Chicago Urban League inner city high schools, Loyola Law School, Chicago, IL

November 15: "OMG, I Have A Case In U.S. Tax Court! A Tax Court Basics Program, Part II," panelist, live webinar, ABA Judicial Division & ABA Center for Professional Division

November 27: Florida Tax Bar, Tax Section, Tampa, FL

December 13: "Wisdom Across the Generations," panelist, ABA 35th Annual National Institute on Criminal Tax Fraud & 8th Annual National Institute on Tax Controversy, Las Vegas, NV

2019

January 23: "Education and Diversity", panelist, ABA Judicial Division Standing Committee on Diversity in the Judiciary, Las Vegas Academy of Arts High School, Las Vegas, NV

March 7: "My Career Path from High School to the U.S. Tax Court," Fox Tech Health and Law Professions Magnet High School, San Antonio, TX

March 27: University of the Incarnate Word (Tax Research Class), San Antonio, TX

August 7: "Education and Diversity," panelist, ABA Judicial Division, Hastings Law School, San Francisco, CA

September 12: Panelist on tax careers, Texas Tech Law School, Lubbock, TX

October 22: "How to Try Your Best Case Before the Tax Court," Federal Bar Association of Kansas City, MO

2020

January 6–7: "The U.S. Tax Court," luncheon speaker, TXCPA-Houston Foundation 2020 Tax Expo, Sugarland, TX

January 23: "Lessons from the Tax Court Bench," State Bar of Texas-Tax Section-Leadership Academy, San Antonio, TX

February 12: "Path to the Bench," panelist, ABA Judicial Division Committee on Diversity in the Judiciary, Austin, TX

February 12: "Education and Diversity," panelist, ABA Judicial Division Standing Committee of Diversity in the Judiciary, Gonzalo Garza Independent High School, Austin, TX

February 19: "My Career Path from High School to the U.S. Tax Court," Fox Tech Health and Law Professions Magnet High School, San Antonio, TX

October 7: "Making Your Case in the Tax Court—Advocacy Tips," panelist, two virtual webinars, ABA Judicial Division

October 8: "Pathway to the U.S. Tax Court," speaker, virtual webinar, Dusheyne Academy of the Sacred Heart, 8th grade class, Houston, TX

Judge Vasquez's Law Clerks, Interns, and Externs

Law Clerks

1. Gary Colton (1995–1997), University of Houston
2. Mark Filpi (1995–1996), Georgetown University
3. Mark Perla (1996–1998), New York University
4. Dave Rifkin (1997–1999, 2001–2009), New York University
5. Misti Bridges (1998–2000), New York University
6. Ivan Morales (1999–2001), New York University
7. Brant Hellwig (2000–2001), New York University
8. Amy Wei (2001–2003), New York University
9. Javier Salinas (2003), University of Houston
10. Deborah Karet (2003–2004), New York University
11. Dan White (2004–2005), New York University
12. Jennifer Gurevitz (2005–2006), New York University
13. Max Levine (2006–2007), New York University
14. Jonathan Kalinski (2007–2009), New York University
15. Kimberly Anderson (2008–2009), New York University
16. Jeremy Abrams (2009–2011), New York University
17. Niki Wilkinson (2009–2010), Georgetown University
18. Michael Tosi (2010), New York University
19. Brian Spiegel (2010–2012), New York University
20. Teresa Abney (2011–2013), New York University
21. Ben Friedman (2012–2014), New York University
22. James Yu (2013–2015), New York University
23. Adrian Ochoa (2014–2016), New York University
24. Ayesha Lewis (2015–2016), New York University
25. Leo Unzeitig (2016–2017), Georgetown University

26. Roger Mahon (2016–present), New York University
27. Sarah Gelfand (2017–2019), New York University
28. Tania Alonzo (2019–2020), University of Houston

Interns/Externs

1. Paul McCord (1996), intern, Georgetown University
2. Eddy Arista (1997), summer intern, University of Miami
3. Ruth Tseng (1998), spring intern, Georgetown University
4. Javier Salinas (1998), summer intern, University of Houston (became a law clerk #9)
5. James Brittain (2000), summer intern, University of Houston
6. Scott Kazem (2001), spring extern, George Mason University
7. Kai Kramer (2004), summer intern, University of Houston
8. Charles Galloway (2004), summer intern, University of Houston
9. Tricia Riviere (2005), summer intern, Nova Southeastern University (former trial clerk)
10. James Brown (2006), summer intern, University of Houston
11. Rodney Read (2007), summer intern, University of Houston
12. Paul Wingo (2008), summer intern, University of Houston
13. Melissa Smith (2008), summer intern, University of Houston
14. Mysti Dennis (2008), summer intern, University of Houston
15. Sabastien Chain (2009), summer intern, University of Houston
16. Xenia Wright (2010), spring intern, Howard University
17. Renee Huey (2010), summer intern, New York University
18. Mikhail "Misha" Lopez (2010), summer intern, University of California, Berkeley
19. Scott Klein (2011), spring extern, Georgetown University
20. Justin Krawitz (2011), fall extern, Georgetown University
21. Adam Meeham (2012), spring extern, Georgetown University

22. Rebecca Sager (2012), fall extern, Georgetown University
23. Miriam Song (2013), spring extern, Georgetown University
24. Kieone Cochran (2013), summer intern. University of Houston
25. Jeff Romero (2014), spring extern. George Washington University
26. Sheena Shaghaghi (2014), summer intern, University of Houston
27. Audrey Huffman (2014), fall extern, Georgetown University
28. Alex Sanchez (2015), spring extern, George Washington University
29. Fatima Garcia (2015), summer intern, University of Illinois at Chicago
30. Ephraim Lucas (2015), summer intern, University of Houston
31. Leo Unzeitig (2016), spring intern, Georgetown University (became law clerk #25)
32. John-Michael Speranza (2016), summer intern, University of Houston
33. Veronica Escobedo (2016), fall extern, Georgetown University
34. Shelley Hahn (2017), spring extern, American University Washington
35. Tania Alonzo (2017), fall intern, University of Houston (became law clerk #28)
36. Ibrahim Basit (2017), volunteer, Georgetown University
37. Paolo Olavario (2017), volunteer, Georgetown University
38. Heena Kepadia (2018), spring intern, University of Houston
39. Daizia McGhee (2018), summer intern, University of Houston
40. Scott Lee (2018), fall extern, Georgetown University
41. Sarah Husbands (2019), summer intern, University of Houston
42. Courtney Cooper (2019), summer extern, Suffolk University
43. Rahat Tariq (2020), spring extern, Georgetown University
44. Sam Hamer (2020), fall extern, Georgetown University
45. Andrew Dagen (2020), volunteer, Washington & Lee University

In Memoriam

Leonard Leighton, August 13, 1937 – January 13, 2013
First and only private practice employer, friend, and mentor.

Dr. Ariel Hernandez, January 11, 1948 – April 2, 2013
Physician, cousin, and friend who had a vision of Juan's contribution to society.

Professor Ira B. Shepard, December 14, 1937 – March 27, 2016
Professor Emeritus, University of Houston Law Center, Houston, Texas; friend and mentor.

Judge Howard Dawson, October 23, 1922 – July 15, 2016
U.S. Tax Court-Washington, D.C. Appointed on August 21, 1962; former chief judge and longest-serving judge of the United States Tax Court. Friend, mentor, and supporter of this book.

Gloria Berban, January 18, 1927 – June 14, 2018
Moses Berban, Sr., May 12, 1927 – February 20, 2019
Very dear friends.

Judge David Laro, March 3, 1942 – September 21, 2018.
United States Tax Court, Washington, D.C.-November 2, 1992 – September 21, 2019. Appointed on November 2, 1992; served on the Court until his death. Friend and colleague.

Discussion Guide

By Mary Theresa Vasquez

1. What is the main idea that you get in reading this book?
2. What do you think about the obstacles and challenges that Juan Vasquez faced as a child? List and discuss them.
3. Consider these obstacles and challenges; close your eyes and imagine how you would have been able to handle these.
4. How do you believe that you can mentor and encourage others, most especially children, about their futures and, most specifically, their careers?

Photographs

Juan Reyes Vasquez and Victoria Resendez Vasquez (paternal grandparents), 1950s.

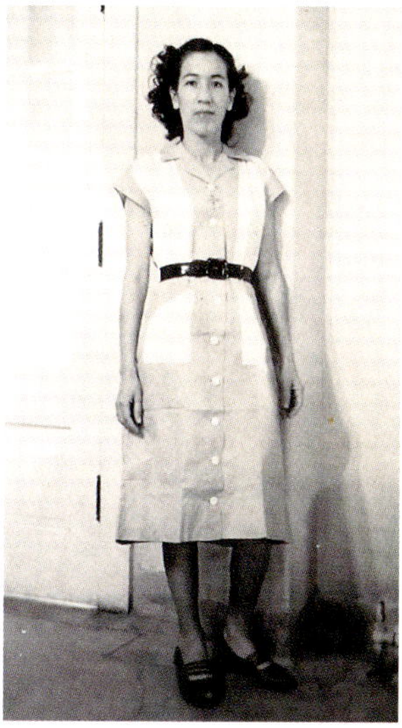

Amelia Flores Vasquez (mother), State Tuberculosis Sanitorium, Carlsbad, Texas, April 5, 1950.

The Vasquez siblings, June 4, 1950 (from left): José Jr., Raymundo, Sylvia, and Juan.

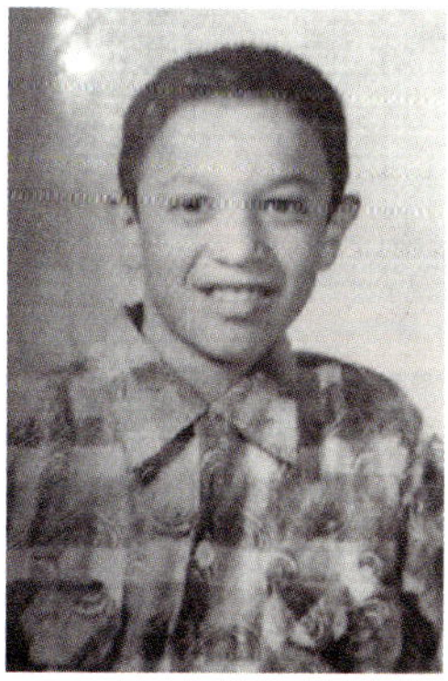

Juan Vasquez, José Navarro Elementary School, 1957-1958 school year.

Jesus Jimenez Flores and Basilia Hernandez Flores (maternal grandparents), 1950s.

Cotton field shack with quarters for three families. Picture taken summer 1988 by Mary Theresa Vasquez.

Juan at age 14 standing next to Don Trini Encino's truck, 1962.

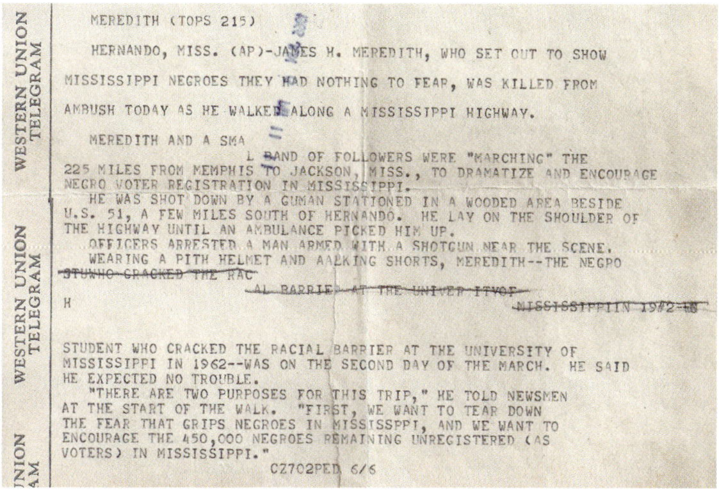

WESTERN UNION TELEGRAM

MEREDITH (TOPS 215)

HERNANDO, MISS. (AP)-JAMES H. MEREDITH, WHO SET OUT TO SHOW MISSISSIPPI NEGROES THEY HAD NOTHING TO FEAR, WAS KILLED FROM AMBUSH TODAY AS HE WALKED ALONG A MISSISSIPPI HIGHWAY.

MEREDITH AND A SMA
L BAND OF FOLLOWERS WERE "MARCHING" THE 225 MILES FROM MEMPHIS TO JACKSON, MISS., TO DRAMATIZE AND ENCOURAGE NEGRO VOTER REGISTRATION IN MISSISSIPPI.

HE WAS SHOT DOWN BY A GUMAN STATIONED IN A WOODED AREA BESIDE U.S. 51, A FEW MILES SOUTH OF HERNANDO. HE LAY ON THE SHOULDER OF THE HIGHWAY UNTIL AN AMBULANCE PICKED HIM UP.

OFFICERS ARRESTED A MAN ARMED WITH A SHOTGUN NEAR THE SCENE.

WEARING A PITH HELMET AND AALKING SHORTS, MEREDITH--THE NEGRO ~~STUNHO CRACKED THE RAC~~
~~AL BARRIER AT THE UNIVER ITYOF~~
H ~~MISSISSIPPIIN 1962-46~~

WESTERN UNION TELEGRAM

STUDENT WHO CRACKED THE RACIAL BARRIER AT THE UNIVERSITY OF MISSISSIPPI IN 1962--WAS ON THE SECOND DAY OF THE MARCH. HE SAID HE EXPECTED NO TROUBLE.

"THERE ARE TWO PURPOSES FOR THIS TRIP," HE TOLD NEWSMEN AT THE START OF THE WALK. "FIRST, WE WANT TO TEAR DOWN THE FEAR THAT GRIPS NEGROES IN MISSISSPPI, AND WE WANT TO ENCOURAGE THE 450,000 NEGROES REMAINING UNREGISTERED (AS VOTERS) IN MISSISSIPPI."

CZ702PED 6/6

Western Union teletype of Associated Press news announcement of the shooting of James Meredith, June 6, 1966.

Terry Schultz and Juan Vasquez, senior prom, Louis W. Fox Vocational and Technical High School, spring 1967.

Juan Vasquez graduates from Louis W. Fox Vocational and Technical High School, May 18, 1967.

Juan and Terry's wedding day, with Jesus and Basilia Flores (left) and Reyes and Mary Ruth Schultz (right). August 22, 1970.

Juan and Terry's home, August 1970 to May 1972, University of Texas Trailer Park, lot number 65.

Juan and son Juan Jr., New York City, 1977-1978.

Shoveling snow in Buffalo, New York, winter 1974-1975.

First judicial appointment hearing before the Senate Finance Committee, February 16, 1995. From left, Juan F. Vasquez, U.S. Representative Frank Tejeda, and U.S. Senator Kay Bailey Hutchinson.

The Vasquez family, 1982.

U.S. Representative Henry B. González with, from left, Jaime, Juan Jr., and Juan Sr., February 17, 1995.

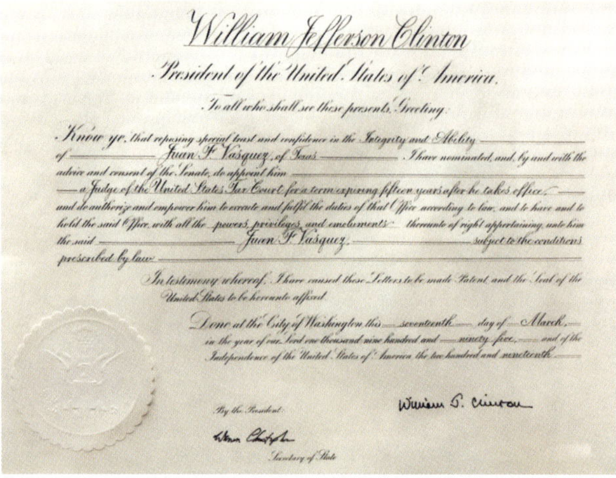

William Jefferson Clinton

President of the United States of America.

To all who shall see these presents, Greeting:

Know ye, that reposing special trust and confidence in the Integrity and Ability of Juan F. Vasquez, of Texas, I have nominated, and, by and with the advice and consent of the Senate, do appoint him a Judge of the United States Tax Court for a term expiring fifteen years after he takes office, and do authorize and empower him to execute and fulfil the duties of that Office according to law, and to have and to hold the said Office, with all the powers, privileges, and emoluments thereunto of right appertaining, unto him the said Juan F. Vasquez, subject to the conditions prescribed by law.

In testimony whereof, I have caused these Letters to be made Patent and the Seal of the United States to be hereunto affixed.

Done at the City of Washington this seventeenth day of March, in the year of our Lord one thousand nine hundred and ninety five, and of the Independence of the United States of America the two hundred and nineteenth.

By the President: William J. Clinton

Secretary of State

Presidential commission of Juan F. Vasquez to the United States Tax Court, March 17, 1995.

Juan in San Antonio office, packing for move to Washington, D.C., 1995.

Formal investiture as judge of the U.S. Tax Court, May 5, 1995. Judge Thomas B. Wells swears in Juan, with Terry holding the Bible.

Los Piscadores *depicts Juan at age 10 and his maternal grandfather, Don Jesus Flores. Acrylic on canvas, 82 inches x 48 inches, 1985, Jesse Treviño. Used by permission.*

American Dream, *lefthand segment, with Judge Juan F. Vasquez at the top, third from left. Mural, Mi Tierra Café y Panadería, San Antonio, Texas, 1990-present, Jesus Garza and Robert Ytuarte. Used by permission of MTC Inc.*

The Vasquez family at the U.S. Tax Court, May 11, 2017. From left, Jaime, Terry, Juan Sr., and Juan Jr.

Viva Fiesta *depicts Juan and Terry Vasquez surrounded by family and friends, enjoying the annual Fiesta Flambeau Parade. Acrylic on canvas, 62 inches x 50 inches, 2010, Jesse Treviño. Used by permission.*